SCRAPS BUILD A PILE

Published by Whirlwind Press

Illustrations by Priska Wenger Mage
Cartoons by John Klossner
Book design by Studio Maria Mayer Feng, LLC

ISBN: 979-8-9909453-2-6

Printed in California

For Richard

who was there
every step of the way

SCRAPS BUILD A PILE

FORGING A PATH IN SILICON VALLEY COMMERCIAL REAL ESTATE

PATTY MCGUIGAN

WHIRLWIND PRESS
INDEPENDENT AUTHORS

TABLE OF CONTENTS

INTRODUCTION

From studying on the UCLA campus to teaching literature to students in Los Angeles Unified School District, this SoCal Valley girl always had a spark of sales in her Irish soul. Given a surprise divorce and the necessities of motherhood, Patty McGuigan wiped her tears, packed up her bags, and relocated with her children Christopher and Diana to Northern California. This life-changing move took guts, moxie, and a winner-takes-all attitude. Fortunately, Patty had those qualities in spades, and quickly found a sales job in San Francisco, which was the genesis of a new career.

Patty is blessed with an unparalleled energy and an enormous amount of stamina. These qualities, coupled with the ability to create good relationships, made her a full sales package. Commercial real estate mirrored the high-tech boom as the internet and cell phones invaded our lives. She bravely chose to go where few women had gone before and joined the key real estate firm Cornish & Carey. Patty needed no permission. She was intractable and fast on her way to becoming the "Grand Dame" of commercial real estate. Unconventional and full of fun, frivolity, and outside-the-box thinking, she turned her scraps into an enormous pile.

As a student of the world, her classroom was travel whenever she could eke out the time. This high-octane life required refueling, which she found in her love of reading, drawing, and the sanctuary of her beach house. Richard "Dick" Bush, her second husband, became her rudder and a guiding force in life and in business. As a bonus, he was almost as colorful as Patty, with an unmatched sense of humor.

Oh, there were ups and downs in the market, dot-com bubbles and bursts, and currently AI has emerged as the new new thing. Techies can now work from anywhere and commercial real estate needs are changing.

Patty has received numerous awards throughout her career, from the "Rookie of the Year" award to "Woman of Influence in the Bay Area," to the prestigious Russ Thomson award for team leadership and community involvement. She made "Top 10 Realtor" (for altogether 15 years) and was the first woman ever induced into the NAIOP (Commercial Real Estate Development Association) Hall of Fame.

Since the passing of her beloved soulmate Dick, she has taken more time to unveil her creative side. Patty has authored and published several books, and continues living her life to the fullest. And yet… she keeps the sales spark burning. To date, Patty has completed 1,896 deals.

– Suzette Dammier

AND SO IT BEGAN

When I plunged into my career in commercial real estate in 1980, the tech wave in what was later going to be Silicon Valley was gathering momentum. It was the home of the developers who rode the highs and lows of the economy and caught the big wave of the technology boom in California.

Rewind back to 1976. I was living my life under the blue skies of Southern California to the background music of the Beach Boys and the Eagles. My days were busy: I was married, with two kids in school, and working as a part-time teacher. I was biking, playing tennis, and having get-togethers with friends and their kids. Then, suddenly, the rug was pulled out from under my feet... my husband of thirteen years asked me for a divorce. That, and a train of daunting events followed: I was transferred to a school fifty miles away in a really problematic part of Los Angeles, the house we lived in was unaffordable on a teacher's salary, and then, on top of it, my car blew up. I was naive, but I assessed my situation and knew I had to get another career.

I read the book *What Color Is Your Parachute* by Richard Nelson Bolles, a self-help book for job-seekers on how to take your skills and reinvent them for a new path. And a priest with whom I was talking gave me some good advice: "An opportunity is an inconvenience well received." That quotation from G.K. Chesterton became my mantra for living my life. With those two pieces of wisdom and the fact that I couldn't type, I came to the conclusion that sales had to be my calling. I was aggressive, liked the tenets of sales and the results. All in all, it appeared to be a flexible enough career where I could raise my kids and make a great living. I learned quickly. I began what became the big reconstruction of my life: Patty 2.0.

I moved to the Bay Area, took back my wonderful Irish name, got an entry level sales job selling fax machines, bought a townhouse, put the kids in new schools, and married a wonderful man named Richard.

Fast-forward to 1980, the year that marked the final step in turning my life around. I was still naive, but I was curious, energetic, and enthusiastic. I took the leap into a career in commercial real estate. I dove in and didn't look back—or even blink. I was hired by a commercial real estate company named Cornish & Carey in Santa Clara (soon to be known as Silicon Valley). I knew nothing about real estate, technology, or Santa Clara. I didn't even know how agents got paid. I just knew they made more money than an office product salesperson. I got my real estate license and was only the second woman hired in a twenty-five-man office. It didn't daunt me, but it certainly daunted the men.

Sales are sales and I knew how to sell. I was a quick learner, full of energy, audacious and unstoppable. I got started, first with the scraps the men in my office didn't want. I called on every kind of business, learned the real estate vocabulary, made countless deals, worked on anything that moved.

Commercial real estate is a deal transaction business and every deal needs an advocate. That person in real estate is the broker. A client needs space for his business. The broker collects a list of spaces that could work for that business which details location, availability, size, price. The broker prepares an offer that includes the terms and the financial information that shows the tenant is able to pay the rent.

That all sounds simple, but each of those elements is laden with twists and turns. A broker explains, cajoles, adjusts all those deal points until both parties agree. That is the essence of a deal. Each completed deal was a scrap.

During those years building my pile, I had quite a collection of wonderful adventures. I worked with crazy, brilliant, quirky people and collected marvelous stories along the way. So, here we go on this magical mystery saga of commercial real estate through the eyes of a wild Irish lass.

Lots of scraps of all shapes and sizes, collected over forty-four years, made my pile. Over the decades, the pile turned into millions.

"I PROMISE YOU, MA'AM – YOU'RE THE FIRST REALTOR ON THIS PROJECT."

PENNIES TO TRACK MY PILE

I just jumped in since I knew the sales process from selling office products, and I started cold calling. I can honestly say no one is as good as I am at cold calling. I think of it in terms of shopping. I would call on businesses, ask for a president or manager, so that I knew that I would be talking to someone in charge. I'd explain that I was there to help them find a new location if they were growing. I filed the cards, keeping the ones of businesses that looked like they were bustling, followed up, made appointments, found spots that fit their growing needs. It was nothing for me to do thirty to forty calls a day.

When I was at UCLA, in education classes in the early sixties, the theme for every lesson plan was behavioral objectives—learning to measure everything and tracking the data. We didn't call it that, but that is what we were taught.

That bit of educational advice stuck with me. I, who never had a balanced checkbook, kept track of what is important to me. Obviously, the balance of the checkbook is not important to me, but I did know how to create measurable objectives for what I thought mattered.

I learned sales begins as a numbers game. I had to make calls, get appointments, figure out the need, fill the need, close the deal. I created a scheme.

I put ten pennies on one side of the phone. Every time I connected with someone I moved a penny. I did not go home until I had moved all ten pennies. It was a simple, straightforward program. It worked. It built a book of business. I followed it religiously. It may not work for others, but it worked for me.

It seemed to me a simple formula to run a sales day, and it worked wonders in real estate. I learned how to qualify a potential client. I learned how to ask for the order. I learned how to close a deal. Frankly, I marvel that people are so intrigued with my scheme.

It's straightforward and leads to results. I would find someone who needed a space in which to work, he'd select an available space, sign a lease, deal done. End of statement. That process led to lots of scraps for the pile.

In the 80s, that simple plan developed into an enormous amount of business. We all were at ground zero in Silicon Valley, laying the foundation for the Digital Age that determined how we would live, work, and communicate.

We were changing the world, and I was doing it one penny at a time.

A SORCERER'S APPRENTICE

A lot of other real estate firms at the time used the concept of internship as an introduction to brokerage. But at Cornish & Carey we called ourselves entrepreneurs, which meant it was much more like the sorcerer's apprentice style. No set program. Ask questions. Learn from your mistakes.

I did slow down when I was putting tours together and when I had to drive to show a space. I did not know the streets well yet, and I wasn't a particularly good driver. Finding the spaces was definitely challenging. There was no GPS and I couldn't read maps very well. More than one client got carsick with my stop-start driving. I do think that helped them make a quicker decision, however. If finding the perfect space meant they had to drive with me to more spaces, they settled quickly for a space that worked. It made for a faster deal.

I had my penny strategy: Contact ten companies a day. A tour a day. A deal a week. After selling a fax machine that nobody needed and really didn't work, this real estate process was far more straightforward and easier to master.

I got the hang of it quickly. This was a great way to make a living. In my early days in Santa Clara, we were far more of the free-range chicken school. People did help each other. There was a camaraderie much like a locker room. None of this got in my way, as I was fascinated with real estate and what these different businesses did. It was easy to get to the president of a company and these companies were growing. This was nirvana for me. After all, I had been selling one little facsimile machine for $39 each in the one ZIP code that was my allocated territory. Now I was selling the whole space for the business and I could call on any ZIP code. I loved it.

So I made my cold calls. I'd share a deal with an agent that I thought might know the territory. Watch, learn, ask questions. It didn't take me long to put this strategy into action.

The Koll Company had four parks called incubator parks. They were small—800 to 2,000 sq ft designed to start a company. They paid $200 to $1000 as a leasing commission for each lease, but they gave the broker a $500 gift certificate for every deal completed. This was perfect for me. I collected over $15,000 dollars of gift certificates that I did not have to share with the company. When I met the president of Koll, I thanked him for supplying me with a clothes budget for the year. He laughed, saying it was the best money he'd ever spent and I looked great. We were all happy.

When my manager said, "Patty. It's time to move on to bigger deals," I heard him. I continued to do these small deals, but I did limit them to my lunch time. After all, this clothes budget program was great fun for me. It took me months to wean myself off that program. I have great fond memories of that time. All this business was so much easier than school teaching.

My rookie year was one of my very favorite years. Sixty deals. $124,000 dollars earned. (More than ten times what I had earned as a teacher.) I was #6 in the top ten of the company. Splendid, and it was great fun.

The scraps were growing at a steady pace. It was starting to look like a pile then.

GORILLA WINS THE DAY

In six months, I had done twenty deals. I asked my manager Steve Mould, "What do I do next?"

He said, "Talk to the owner of any property you've dealt with, and ask him for an exclusive listing to work on. Then you get half of every listing done there." That made sense. In commercial real estate the landlord hires a listing agent to help lease vacant space in the building, and the listing agent earns a commission on every leasing transaction completed. So I wrote up a list of properties and called Birk McCandless, who owned the project on Montague Expressway, which was a large R & D project. He did not return the call.

I called and called and called. Nothing. So I planned another strategy. I didn't ask or tell anyone. I just did it. I hired a person to go to Birk's office dressed as a gorilla with balloons in one hand and my exclusive contract in the other. Birk called, "I guess I have to see you. There's a gorilla in my lobby." I answered, "I'll be right there."

We chatted and after a bit he said, "I have this two-story building on Zanker. I'll give you a listing on that." Two-story buildings were notoriously unpopular in 1980. Land was abundant and it was easy, simple, and fast to build single-story buildings. Engineers liked that. No one was sophisticated and architectural design was unheard of. What more did you need beyond four walls and a roof? Everyone thought democratically in the Valley. They did not like the idea of 'upstairs management.' I also found out later that his father Charles McCandless used to call the building "the pound," because he thought it was only fit for dogs.

So I looked at Birk and said, "I'll take the Zanker building, but only if you give me the Montague project. I know I can lease that. I've done six deals there. I have to make this work or you'll never hire me again. So I'll take Zanker. However, if you're only going to give me one project, it has to be Montague." He mused and then agreed. I walked out of the office—six months in the business with two listings over 100,000 sq ft. I was off and running.

In 2023, over forty years later, Steve Sund, who had worked for Birk for over fifty, sent me a birthday email: "A blinding light switched on when you had to make it on your own. You were not to be ignored. That light has never dimmed or flickered all these years later. Cheers to many more."

I still work with Steve. We have great memories, lots of laughs, and have done hundreds of leases over the past forty-four years.

"THE REALTOR IS HERE TO SEE YOU, SIR."

BUILDING MY BRAND

The best rule of sales—repeat customers.

Holidays gave me an opportunity to market myself and I turned them into a sales production. Christmas at my house was a major production with lots of special happenings.

First thing in December, Advent calendars went out to potential clients' families, over one hundred of them, with a piece of chocolate for every day before Christmas. This way, every day some child asked his father, "Who gave us this chocolate?" And the response would be "Patty."

Second were real estate-focused Christmas cards. My favorite one, for example: Me on my bike in front of a 'for sale' sign in Ireland that read 'Commercial land for sale. Uses—funeral home. Supermarket. Petrol station.'

I had a for sale sign in front of Hampton Court Palace in London. Hampton Court is a historical palace that housed royalty from the 1500s until the late 1700s, and is still owned by the Crown. It at one point was used as the residence for the wives of Henry VIII. We were taking photos with my sale sign. And it read: "If it worked for Henry VIII and his six wives—it will work for you." I almost got arrested for that photo. The English have a rule that no one can use Hampton Court for marketing purposes.

One year my card was a Hawaiian shack—"Your fixer-upper in the perfect location." I became known for these funny and unique cards around the holidays. A real twist on real estate marketing. But it certainly was a job to get them all out.

In the early days of brokerage, we had these senior management meetings. One was in December. December is a dreadful month for a woman—Christmas tree, shopping, wrapping presents, plus regular workload, and then the family still needs food and clean clothes. Dreadful month, every moment counted. I privately thought these meetings were worthless. So I took my Christmas cards in and addressed them during the meeting. I was the ultimate multitasker. I did have one manager who was really unnerved by my Christmas card addressing. He must have been flabbergasted that someone had the guts to do something else during this meeting. However, he was not responsible for family meals and clean clothes. His wife addressed his Christmas cards.

St. Patrick's Day was a national holiday for me, being Irish. I'd dressed up in a green hat and other Irish paraphernalia. I'd spend the day delivering green cupcakes and St. Patty's goodwill to clients.

And that was how the year evolved and how I rolled! I was like the Hallmark card of real estate—always in costume delivering something to somebody. The message was: 'Remember me—I'm the real estate lady,' and I made sure everyone in their respective company felt allegiance to me whenever they needed some space.

Silly. Creative. Exhausting, but it worked. These outside-of-the-box methods created more scraps that built the pile.

BARNUM & BAILEY

First year in the business and I knew I'd found a career I loved. Selling real estate simply fit the way my mind worked. We didn't have the term back then but I always joke that ADHD was invented to fit my brain.

I loved it so much that after eight months I called Ann Adrian. She was a marvelous friend and colleague of mine who had been my partner in crime selling office products with me at our previous company. Our fax sales were high on marketing and low on functionality and proper engineering. We could talk a good game, but the product never really worked as intended and that's a problem when you're selling a product.

When I discovered commercial real estate, I called Ann, "You have got to come down here. This business is terrific. Instead of selling a small machine, we sell the whole building and there are no moving parts, no products to schlep around or ship."

So Ann came down from San Francisco a year later and was promptly hired and together we combed the 'hood.' Ann also knew how to cold-call and we turned up opportunity after opportunity. We quickly discovered that this real estate was like a circus and we needed to know all of the performers.

We continued to be partners in crime for twenty-five more years.

"THE MORE PHONES I HAVE, THE BETTER MY CHANCES OF MAKING A SALE."

THE QUEEN OF THE SOBRATO EMPIRE

Annie Sobrato was the mother of a young man who would soon become one of the largest builders in Silicon Valley. So Ann Adrian set up lunch for the three of us. We were going to talk business.

Annie was a generation older than we were. And her story was spellbinding. During this lunch, she told us her real estate story.

She had been born and was living in Italy when John Sobrato Sr. came back to his home country to claim her as his bride. She was beautiful and quite a bit younger than John. He married her and brought her from Italy to a new home to the Bay Area. At the time, he had a restaurant in San Francisco, but he did not want his young wife and son living in a city with earthquakes. So he bought a big piece of land in Atherton.

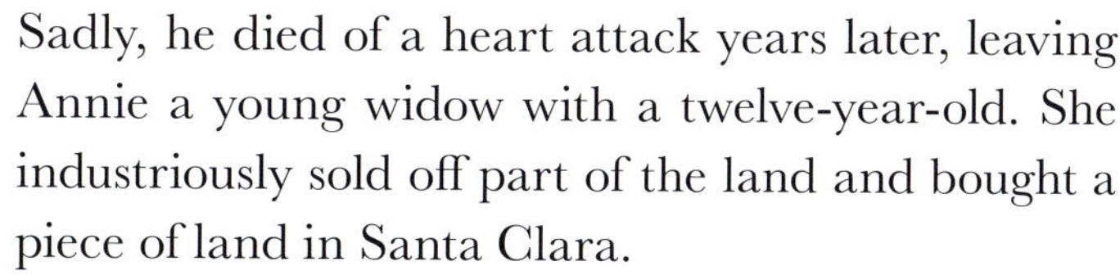

Sadly, he died of a heart attack years later, leaving Annie a young widow with a twelve-year-old. She industriously sold off part of the land and bought a piece of land in Santa Clara.

She then went over to Kaiser Permanente in the East Bay and wrangled a meeting to present this land and propose to build a building for Kaiser. She indeed was the first woman in the Silicon Valley real estate world, she was gorgeous, and no one was going to refuse her. She built the building, which led to eighteen more. One incredible story.

By the time her son John was twenty-one, she had nineteen buildings as his legacy. John met Carl Berg who later became his partner in commercial real estate. As young men, the two of them sold residential houses with Annie as their guiding hand.

Eventually Carl and John divided their properties and set up their own individual companies. Annie was quite a package and wanted to continue to be involved, but her son was moving fast and breaking pace.

One of my favorite stories ever was years later when the market was on a down cycle. John and his own son John Michael had a 20,000-sq-ft building in Sunnyvale that included Annie in the ownership. The market was wobbly and they had given six months of free rent to get the tenant into the property. The deal was signed, but as a formality they needed Annie's signature as well. She said she was not giving any tenant free rent and she was not about to sign the lease. John went crazy. He explained this was the market and this was how deals were done these days. Annie held her ground. So John and John Michael personally paid her the free rent to get the deal completed. I understand the predicament, but I was so amused by it all I could only laugh. She was a full-fledged character with abundant energy and she shared a love of dealmaking.

John was on a rocket ride and became one of the most successful developers in Silicon Valley. He built an empire. He was a superb dealmaker, but his mother was there to remind him of his beginnings.

At the lunch when I met Annie, her grandson John Michael came over to have a Diet Coke and see his grandmother and her friends. He was twenty years old and was setting up a computer system for the company. Without the Sobrato name, John Michael would more than likely have worked at Apple and been a key part of the Apple empire, but he was a Sobrato, the only boy. He chose to work with his dad and played an integral part in building that real estate empire.

After lunch, I stopped by the Sobrato office to introduce myself to John Sobrato and to tell him I'd just had lunch with his mother. He told me forthrightly, "Don't think this is going to do you any good. Get to work and find a tenant for me."

Over the years, I did find tenants for them. John Michael and his wife became friends of mine and I can say John Michael brought civility and business etiquette to the Sobrato Organization. Their philanthropy has enormously touched all parts of the community and their buildings have housed many of the best firms in the Valley.

I'd like to remind everyone that Annie started that ball rolling as a widow with a child and a piece of land. Bravo. Job well done—to all of them!

Chop Keenan

John Sobrato

John Arrillaga

Ned Spieker

John Mozart

Carl Berg

David Brown

Richard Peery

Jim Mair

THE MAGNIFICENT SEVEN

The NAIOP (Commercial Real Estate Development Association) supports and honors the commercial real estate development industry by providing advocacy, education, research, and connections to foster business opportunities.

In 2007, the Silicon Valley chapter created a Hall of Fame to celebrate the pioneering industry leaders who built spaces for tech entrepreneurs to start a digital revolution. The first recipients of the award were Richard Peery and John Arrillaga, followed by John A. Sobrato in 2008, David Brown, Sr. in 2009, Carl E. Berg in 2010, Warren "Ned" Spieker, Jr. in 2011, Charles "Chop" Keenan III in 2013, John Mozart in 2015, and Jim Mair in 2017. All were commercial real estate developers except for Chop Keenan, who built the houses for everyone in tech.

Destined to lead, these industry titans (all born between 1935 and 1945) grew up in the area, attended college, got married, and raised families. If they ever worked for anyone else, it wouldn't have been for very long. Think of the movie *The Magnificent Seven*; this was a wild bunch! Each one brought his unique personality and vision to real estate development. All creative, smart, and high-risk-taking entrepreneurs, they built a world that didn't exist before. They knew what they wanted to get done, and by hook or by crook, they pulled it off. Real once-in-a-lifetime characters, and I got to know and to work with them all. Lucky me!

This book would not be complete without their stories. After all, these men wove the fabric that I used as scraps to build my career.

JOHN ARRILLAGA & RICHARD PEERY: THE GOLD STANDARD

These two men were quite a pair. The only partnership of the Magnificent Seven, and it lasted until John's death in 2022. They had different backgrounds, attended different colleges, and had very separate and unique skills. John and Dick were not particularly close personal friends, yet together as businessmen they were invincible. They were certainly the leaders of the pack, had partnerships with other developers, and had countless relationships in all parts of the business world. I repeat—invincible.

Dick was brilliant in land. He knew what to buy, when to buy it, how to finance if he needed to; he was bulletproof. John was the quintessential salesman. He designed the building for maximum flexibility with a simple classic design for longevity. His "Lego blocks" were gold.

John had ironclad control of the entire building process. He'd start his day at five in the morning, checking the sites. He knew his tenants, and grew them from one building to another. He took over all the planning of the building for his properties so that all his tenant had to do was sign the lease. His prices were outrageous but he delivered, and the companies could grow at an incredible pace without giving any thought to housing the company as John "took care of them." It all worked.

I must say writing this is a bit of a challenge as I am a broker and John hated all brokers, though he himself had started as a broker. For him, brokerage had been simply a stepping stone. He called us "expensive taxi drivers" and his commission fee was stingy. As Perry and Arrillaga built their empire, brokers were definitely personas non grata.

DAVID & GOLIATH SILICON VALLEY STYLE

One of Ann Adrian and my favorite projects was with a company called Tiburon Systems which developed technology for the Air Force and law enforcement. Ann had found Jere Patterson who was leaving Lockheed, a Tiburon competitor, with his entire team. They needed a space that was small, cheap, and short term since they hadn't secured any funding yet. We found Jere 2,700 sq ft for 85 cents per sq ft a month for a year. He thought we were magic. We just might have been magic then.

Jere looked at the space and said, "I'll take it." Then we discovered there were twenty-seven of them. There was no remote working at this time. These fellows almost filled the space standing up. How were we ever going to get desks, computers, and a coffee pot into this space (thank heavens bathrooms were already in)?

Jere looked at us reassuringly. "We 'hot-desk' it." They all wouldn't be in on the same day at the same time. Jere had been in the military service. He said "hot-bedding it" was a common occurrence. You slept where and when you could. There were never enough beds for everyone on his ship. Same thing was true in an office. They just needed the space until they got "the contract." That contract would be their funding. They never needed venture capital. A solid contract with the government was sufficient credit to secure a building. Then they'd move. Made sense to us. We liked the fact they'd need to move. More scraps for the pile.

In their space, they all started working on the response to a special government contract that required high-security engineers. These twenty-seven were up against Lockheed. How were they possibly going to win that contract? Easy—Jere's team was the only group in the Valley that had sufficient numbers of this particular high-clearance security ranking. Jere knew this when he had left Lockheed. Brilliant, and only in the Valley could he ever have corralled the fellows, found the space, and commandeered the contract. Yes, and he did it all right under the nose of Lockheed.

The next speed bump for us was, he needed a space with a SCIF. "What is a SCIF?" we asked.

SCIF, we learned, is a Sensitive Compartmented Information Facility, a secure room that guards against electronic surveillance and suppresses data leakage of sensitive military and security information. In layman's terms, it was a lead box that nothing could penetrate. No one could get at the information (aka data) that was in the room.

Hmmm… this could be challenging. Remember, many of Silicon Valley's first forays into technology were with government contracts. To our surprise, the SCIFs were around. We just had to find one that was discarded. We originally thought this was "Mission Impossible"—a room with no windows and steel walls. Sounded like a jail to us. However, there was one available. Jere got 'the contract' and the gang moved into the facility.

Jere had great managerial skills. He was straightforward, clear-thinking, fair, not egotistical, and he knew his market. Great CEO ingredients.

We moved them four more times. Finally, they landed in west San Jose in a 100,000-sq-ft building that remained their headquarters. It was eventually sold to Texas Instruments. Jere had made enough money that he was able to enjoy his boat. He no longer had to 'hot-bed' or 'hot-desk it.' He had his own bed on his own boat and his own slip to park it in.

My pile grew commensurately.

"I THINK I SEE THE PROBLEM. YOU JUST ANSWERED YOUR WALLET."

PARTNERS IN CRIME

Over the years, I've had lots of business partners. For me, I found it far more entertaining, a better use of resources, and less stressful to work a deal with a partner.

I knew my skill set and I knew my weaknesses. Partnering was perfect for me. I could always find a deal. I could close a deal. It was the driving to and finding the property where I could use help. Phil Trautman was a perfect match. A slightly older, distinguished, highly intelligent man who had graduated from Rensselaer as an engineer, but really just wanted to be his own boss. Somehow he'd found commercial real estate. He was not a salesman, but he was perfect for me. We were great together.

Somehow we had gotten wind of a potential deal on an old house in a commercial area on Alum Rock in East San Jose. The area was certainly not the tech world and a bit rough.

In his big blue Cadillac, we drove up to this sketchy house on a corner next to a business that made monument headstones for cemeteries, which was perfect since the cemetery was just on the other side of the property. Hmmm, the house was boarded up and appeared not to have been lived in for a good long while. Phil had stopped at a hardware store and bought a hammer. After tearing off the boards that covered the door and the windows, he simply inserted the key and the door opened. At this point, I walked in front of him and burst into the house. Phil quietly looked at me and said, “Did you ever think there might have been a body in here?”

Of course that thought had never entered my mind. Typical of me, I had only one speed: fast. I had barged in to see what we had there. And what we had there was a real challenge. We were way out of the comfort zone of commercial real estate. But a deal was a deal. One of the tenets of real estate is “stand on the roof and you’ll see your next buyer.” So we went next door to the monument headstone business. The owner didn’t need any more space nor could he give us any ideas about who might need that building for anything. This really had to be the deadest property I’d ever had. Surprisingly, we did sell it for $99,000. We were shocked anyone would buy it. The fact that it sold was amazing.

We left that street, never to return. Phil did look it up years later and it had resold for $105,000. This was definitely not in the burgeoning Silicon Valley tech world. I made a note to myself—leave south of downtown San Jose to other brokers. Do not burst through the door of an abandoned building, and monuments for gravestones are not a fast-growing business. However, this scrap did go on the pile and I’d learned a few life lessons.

A REAL ESTATE TRUTH

You don't necessarily have to have seen the building. You just have to get the lease signed.

Only forty-four years of real estate allows me to be this honest. Full disclosure: for the first deal I made where the commission was over $100,000, I had not seen the building. How could this be? Well, here's how that happened.

It must have been in 1981, Phil Trautman and I had gone cold calling and found a company called Ricoh, a Japanese office product company, that needed to expand. Another fellow in the office, Fred Pilster, had somehow discovered them as well. So, we three joined forces to work on the deal. They needed a 50,000-sq-ft facility—a large requirement then as now. We fleshed out which buildings could fit their needs, time, and location.

At that time, 'facilities fellows' were the contact/first-level decision-makers. They would do the large overview, choose the best of the bunch, and then the president or area manager would review the buildings.

One afternoon the big tour was happening. Each of us went to a building to be sure the tour flow went properly. Ricoh chose Orchard Property owned by Renco. It was a shell building that had to be fitted out. So the process was an involved one, requiring several meetings and lots of decisions.

Finally, we were ready to deliver the lease. Fred was my age, a chauvinist of the first rank, and saw little value in me, though he had only started a year before me.

I quietly told Phil that I had in fact never seen the building nor even knew how to get to said street it was on since it was in San Jose. As I mentioned before, I was not the master of maps and had no sense of direction. Remember, this was my first year and I had not mastered San Jose yet. There were no Google maps, just the Thomas Guide maps, and I frankly was not very good at reading them. If Fred had ever found this out, I would have been relegated to assistant, and treated with great disdain.

Phil quietly said to me, "Let's go for a short drive." We slipped out of the office and down to Orchard Parkway. This was one big building. I was impressed. Wow. I had hit easy street. My scraps were getting larger. In my defense, as the deal progressed, I was the one who worked diligently with the landlord and tenant at the design meetings. Fred and Phil were not very good at design.

Both were delighted. In fact, the developer who normally had a cap of $100,000 on a commission gave us $150,000 because the transaction had gone so smoothly. That was unheard of.

Only today do I tell the world the fact that I had not seen the building I had leased. Phil had earned my love and respect. We went on to do many more deals. I'd dig them up, and he'd make sure I didn't make a fool of myself. Together we were quite a team and pulled off many miracles.

"CAN YOU GUYS LOOK A LITTLE MORE TECH-FRIENDLY?"

THE RWEEESTATE LADY

In the mid-'80s, Televideo, a company founded by the South Korean entrepreneur Philip Hwang, came to Silicon Valley. Philip wanted to build a computer terminal business. As his business grew, he added personal desktop computers to his product line. The company was doing well and needed space. Phil Trautman, Frank Cox, and I got the assignment. The three musketeers were up for the challenge.

Intel no longer needed the 150,000-sq-ft building at Brokow and the 101 because they were consolidating in Santa Clara. The location and size would be a great fit for Televideo. So they bought it and used it for a few years, but then they ran into financial difficulties. Televideo was hit with staggering competition. When they no longer needed this facility, we put it on the market.

The building sat on eight acres but was really a warehouse. Finding a tenant for it was challenging. Every time we had a tour the fellow in charge of the warehouse would get so excited. He'd holler, "The rweeestate lady is here." I felt like I was the Korean version of Santa Claus.

We worked on a potential lease with IKEA. They liked the parking options and location, but they couldn't come to terms with the city of San Jose over tax benefits that they wanted. That deal blew up. However, I got the idea that perhaps there was a market beyond technology for this property. Interesting idea.

Finally, I was touring a broker who was not from any of the commercial offices, but he had a seemingly interested client who carefully made sure not to identify himself. One hundred fifty thousand sq ft is a big building and this one was filled with unsold computer terminals, hundreds of them, row after row after row. Quite a sight. This client got so excited walking through the space. The vastness did not overwhelm him.

A good real estate agent is a good detective. I watched him. He was in love with this building. I didn't know who he was or what his company did, but I knew I had found my buyer. The client was John Fry who owned grocery stores originally but now was adding an array of computer parts to his inventory. As tech grew, he reorganized his inventory to add semiconductor chips that were far more profitable than potato chips.

This use was a perfect fit: fabulous location, lots of parking, high ceilings for lots of computer engineer needs, a veritable grocery store for engineers.

Next, Phil, Frank, and I needed to find a smaller location for Televideo and we found one where they would stay until the mid-'90s. In those years, the life of a tech company was measured in dog years. To survive, tech companies had to constantly develop new products.

In the forty-four years I've been working in the Valley, Intel is the only big company that has stayed vibrant. The chip business is a power-hungry, complex, capital- and time-intensive tech business because, at the end of the day, everything needs a chip. The life and complexity of a chip could be a book all by itself, but I'm not writing that one. I just found the land and the building for them. These two deals provided major scraps for the pile.

DATA VERSUS BUS TOUR

Today we all live and breathe data: vacancy absorption, new construction, rental rates, cap rates, and IRR (internal rate of return).

In the 21st century, we're living in a house of cards with only numbers, numbers, and more numbers. Often common sense, architectural design, and usefulness are buried under a pyramid of numbers.

In the '80s, the world had more of a "see and touch" perspective. The ASBB (Association of South Bay Brokers) sponsored an annual event where we did bus tours to see "the territory."

In 1981, I took my first tour to Almaden Valley and South San Jose, Milpitas, Sunnyvale, Mountain View, and a strangely named park, International Business Park, or IBP.

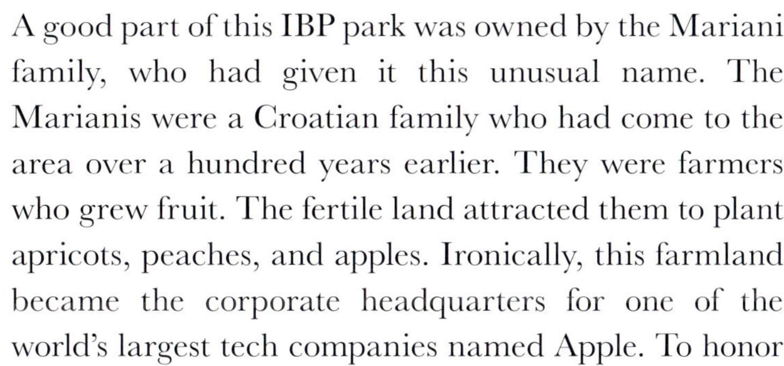

A good part of this IBP park was owned by the Mariani family, who had given it this unusual name. The Marianis were a Croatian family who had come to the area over a hundred years earlier. They were farmers who grew fruit. The fertile land attracted them to plant apricots, peaches, and apples. Ironically, this farmland became the corporate headquarters for one of the world's largest tech companies named Apple. To honor this family, one of the streets in Cupertino is named Mariani Street. To me, it seemed astonishing that anyone, even an entire family, could own such a vast amount of land. On my first tour, it was overwhelming—land, land, and more land.

Again, the Mariani family had come from Croatia to grow fruit in what would become Silicon Valley. But then they got a different, unusual idea for this land. They envisioned a park designated for foreign companies to land in San Jose, work a bit on their new product, and then distribute the product from there throughout the world, thus avoiding the paperwork of customs, taxes, etc. It seemed like a crazy idea to me, but I knew nothing about the distribution of goods or manufacturing or customs regulations. I did realize that the San Jose airport was small and did not have international flights in the '80s. But then there were all sorts of wild ideas flying around Santa Clara County that I didn't quite understand. Incidentally, this idea never came to fruition. However, the airport did triple its size to accommodate the population and economic growth.

Even though the idea of an International Business Park didn't work, the name stuck, and there were several buildings developed there that had to be leased.

Ann Adrian and I got the assignment to lease three of their large impressively monochromatic buildings, each completely tiled in different colors—one blue, one green, one red. These were large, partially two-story, 80,000-sq-ft buildings. When I toured a facility manager who was looking for a building that size, he commented, "With all this tile, I feel I'm in a big bathroom in the sky." These buildings did not have the best architectural design. The location was challenging, size was limiting, and style was unique. One tough assignment, but we did manage it.

When I'd cold-call through the park, I would say, "My name is Patty McGuigan, and the Mariani family asked that I tell you about this building." I sounded like a 'holy roller,' as my mother would say. The name-dropping gave me some advantage, but these buildings were tough to sell.

We did it. I realized, however, if I had to lease space in South San Jose and IBP, my pile would be much slower to grow. I made the decision to save South San Jose for my sixties. Then I rethought it, and moved it to my seventies. One always has to have new territory to look forward to. I eventually dismissed the notion of ever doing a deal this far south. As it turns out, a wise decision, because the core tech business development organically grew around Highway 101 and seemed to stop at the San Jose airport.

The next few years, my tours only covered the core areas from Mountain View to downtown San Jose. Far more manageable. Limiting the territory was a real benefit for me with my driving and directions handicaps.

Often, on these bus tours, I was one of the 'guides.' I am an Irish storyteller and brokers are a great audience. I found these great fun—like Disneyland for the real estate population.

However, we all grew up and decided we no longer needed tours. We simply ate and drank and gave out awards for performances.

I enjoy the pageantry of today's awards ceremony, but I do miss the tales told on the buses.

THE ORIGINAL DATA CENTER

Jim Beeger joined Cornish & Carey in 1982. He was from an old Silicon Valley family and had left a smaller, older commercial firm. His skill set was that of a librarian… he knew all the data about all the buildings in Silicon Valley and he always retained this information in large notebooks and delivered them every quarter. He was a gentleman and an organized scholarly fellow though his family did own a ranch out in the San Jose country and he did hunt. The men in the office liked that.

For about five years, the male members of the Santa Clara R & D division of Cornish & Carey were invited to spend the first weekend in June at Jim's extended family's ranch by Mount Hamilton. The women were quite happy not to be a part of the extended C & C boy's club. (Quite honestly this part of San Jose was far beyond my map. I'm certain I would have ended up in Barstow. Also, I had gone to an all-girls school. Events such as this were foreign to me.)

The price of admission was $40.00 per person and Jim supplied all the food and beer. Sounds simple, but single-handedly shopping for as many as seventeen people was no small task. That sounded worse than making Christmas dinner without any of the reward. Was this a common men's phenomenon? The beer component alone was its own trip to Costco—eighteen cases of beer is a load.

These weekends took on an almost mythical reputation. I suspect the smallest stories were highly exaggerated. I had taught high school boys and I knew how they got carried away with stories. What it really consisted of was a bunch of men/boys of diverse backgrounds, races, religions, political beliefs, etc, all looking for the Wild West adventure they'd dreamed of as kids or teenagers. It was like being a kid again—riding ATVs, fishing, shooting innocent and slow-moving animals as if they were fighting off a group of zombies, telling tall tales into the wee hours having drunk far too much beer.

Monday morning followed; stories grew in the telling. I was always amazed someone hadn't maimed himself. I always felt this could have been the real estate version of *Lord of the Flies*, but then I am often accused of seeing Hollywood in life. Finally, age caught up with them. Wives made plans for them. The work to put it on was staggering. The stories fell into the lore of our wild, crazy Santa Clara days.

For me, I always saw Jim as one of the odd couple characters with this ragtag group. Jim was such a gentleman and his skills didn't quite match with hunting and drinking and exaggerated tall tales of prowess. But he wanted to be one of the boys, I guess.

Every agent has a special talent to grow and develop their business. Jim's special talent was collecting and organizing available and leased property. As we leased more and more property in the Valley, that "data" became an all important component for financing—a component that none of us were good at except Jim. He became invaluable.

Jim always said that I had taught him how to sell, but that he had provided the data that supported the presentations. We were a great twosome—fantasy and fact. His quarterly "notebooks" that took an inordinate amount of research and time to put together were done by calls and research. No data collection or Google or AI devices existed, just plain old fashion research work. He had folks steal information or borrow some from a developer that had received some intel. If you were fair, you brought Jim into a deal and he shared the notebook with the client. Some men felt that was too high a price, to split a commission just for facts. Greed has always been a key ingredient in brokerage. Jim figured out how to manage it and built a long successful career around his research.

Jim continued to be our one and only data-man, a man of fine character and honest values. He eventually left for a less rowdy, more businesslike office.

However, when I did my deals with Jim, my scraps were perfect, neatly cut and perfectly shaped, just like Jim's notebooks, not like the wild, crazy weekends.

THE FIRE TRUCK CAPER

Every broker builds their book of business and their brand even when they don't have any idea they are doing it. John Travis (JT to some of us) was a great example of that in our Santa Clara office. He was literally 'larger than life'—big football player, light on schooling, but the expression 'larger than life' was invented for him. He knew everybody and had a great sense of where the power was. His skill set was perfect for selling real estate to a young unsophisticated Silicon Valley.

Everyone cheered for Stanford even though few brokers had attended the school. JT's tailgate parties were legendary. He had somehow managed to buy a full-blown hook-and-ladder fire truck and that was how he arrived at the games to begin his parties. He would have miniature cow milk bottles, and a generator so he could have power for a blender to serve margaritas in those milk bottles. Then he hired Stanford coeds to serve the milk bottle margaritas. Quite a scene.

No cold calls or extensive market reports for JT. He found his clients at the game by serving them enormous margaritas. He did not discover this marketing strategy in a Stanford marketing class. He had great instincts, marvelous people skills, and knew how to close a deal. It definitely worked. He managed to parlay his skills into an ownership of a building with a developer in the middle of Googleland. Amazing that owning one Google building can support a family for a lifetime.

JT's fire truck supported a great lifestyle, three children and their college expenses, and a fine retirement. Could this have happened anywhere else? I doubt it. I think you had to have the freewheeling climate and lack of any social barriers. You had to be able to roll a huge fire truck onto the Stanford campus and start meeting people. JT was a master at it.

My children met JT forty years ago at one of his famous tailgates. They may have talked to me about real estate before JT, but I doubt it. That fire truck caused a lasting impression. They still talk about it today. It certainly was his entry into a career of lifetime real estate, and he never had to prepare one marketing report. We had no social media or email. Marketing then looked primitive compared to the 21st century. We met people. We set up meetings. We drove people in a car to look at property. We delivered leases and then picked them up when they were signed. Sales and marketing was a person-to-person encounter.

At that time in Silicon Valley, gorillas, marching bands, fire trucks, and nun outfits were all part of the marketing program to get a deal done.

"I'M SORRY—THE ICE CUBES
ARE IN THE OTHER FREEZER."

IS THERE A DEAD BODY HERE?

It was October and every October I did a real mind twist in my head, thinking the world was ending. My business was drying up. I would have no deals next year. Sadly enough, every year, I really believed it.

Somehow, in my cold-call scavenger hunts looking for my next deal, I discovered the Cryogenic Group in a building in Sunnyvale. It was a small 10,000-sq-ft building that this group owned, and when I spoke with them they thought they might sell it. The group was made up of a scientist, a residential broker, and a couple of older businessmen. I went to my buddy Frank Cox and suggested this could be a good little building to get a listing to sell.

Frank and I were great partners in crime. We had done every kind of crazy industrial deal imaginable—a legal marijuana dispensary, an old church, coffins-to-go—you name it. We'd worked on it. Frank was twenty years younger than me, and back then he thought I was a goddess; he did fabulous detailed paperwork with the same sense of urgency to get a deal done that I had.

I loved working with him. He was perfect.

He came from central California, was a hunter, talked fast, got things done. He took my place with the Worn Shoe Award. The award went to the broker who had done the most deals in a year. For years that award went to me. He did one hundred deals a year.

At that time, we asked about cryogenics. We discovered it was a way of taking a dead body, filling it with some special chemicals, and preserving the body.

People would do this for a loved one until there would be an advance in medicine where they could bring the body back, repair the illness, and that person would regain life. Weird, weird, weird… but business is business. They no longer had use for the building and would sell it.

As it turned out, we had to meet the scientist in Oakland off Hegenberger Road, a heavy industrial area. Only Frank would be willing to do this wild, crazy call. We drove in the pouring rain, turned and drove down where a large chemical truck was pulling out. We walked into the building, a bare bones warehouse with a seating area in the front. The scientist was there.

Frank asked if that was where they stored the bodies. The fellow pointed to these stainless steel capsules hanging from the rafters behind us. "They're there, right behind you." There were at least sixty capsules hanging there. "This is where we store and maintain the bodies. The truck that just left brings the chemicals to top them up. We have Mr. Dunbar's parents there and their dog. They want the dog when they come back."

Frank looked calm. His next question was about the cost of cryogenics freezing. "Well, it's $150,000 for the set up and then an additional $25,000 a year for maintenance, storage, and additional chemicals."

I began to think we really had gone off the deep end. If this was what life was coming to, everyone was in sad shape. All the brokers were beginning to disagree on marketing. Sales were down. Selling the Sunnyvale building seemed like a good idea. Then they got the notion they needed to be sure we were the right firm to do this. So we actually had to do a presentation. We worked on it, presented it, but lost it to Grubb & Ellis, another real estate firm. In truth, we were the best qualified. We could sell anything. However, one of the partners had a brother at Grubb & Ellis, so they got the business.

This is the one deal that got away. I really was not that upset. These people were odd, certainly not astute businessmen, and it was just too weird even for me. Frank told me later he'd seen the scientist on a television program in Stockton. By that time, he had cancer and was still advocating this cryogenics as a way to save himself for a return when his cancer was curable.

I found it astonishing where my road in real estate took me—and how my own mind could go to crazy places. That deal distracted me enough to get confidence about forecasting the following year, as I had realized the tech world offered me far more reasonable ways to earn a living. However, I often wonder what happened to those cylinders… and the dog?

WHEN THE CRANE WAS THE CALIFORNIA BIRD

Highway 101 was my daily trail for twenty-five years. In the beginning, I had to memorize the towns in order. Then they became second nature for me. Each city had its character and its trademarks. However, the common sight was the crane. Everywhere I looked, cranes were in motion lifting things up and down. I remember going to lunch with one developer. He said, "We've got to stop by city hall." He walked in, looked at the clerk, and said, "I'll be back Monday for the permit."

She said, "We are working as fast as possible, but it may not be ready until Thursday."

His answer, "Do the best you can, but we're breaking ground on Monday."

We were all full of ourselves. Young, brash, know-it-alls building a new world. Gone were the orchards, in were the tilt-ups. A tilt-up is a type of building and a construction technique using concrete. It is a cost-effective process with a short completion time.

This was the perfect kind of quick construction that suited the focused engineers with a new grand idea. The notion of style or longevity never entered their minds. The buildings became almost disposable as they raced to get the product out the door. No need for an architect nor designers, nor approvals.

Consequently, every day as I drove down the freeway, I'd spot yet another building. I leased one building five times. Every year I'd lease it, then the company would expand. Another company would come in. All five-year leases satisfied the bank's need for financing and each of the companies outgrew the building in a year. Each time I was paid a five-year commission. My husband asked, "Isn't that churning?"

My answer: "It all goes on so quickly the bank is totally confused." Then I'd lease it again. This suited the California mentality. First gold, then silver, now silicon. Everywhere companies were racing to join the digital world. Goodbye telex, hello email. I could do a deal a week without a problem. There were years I had a million sq ft of property under contract to get leased.

My son was a journalist in New Hampshire and called me for an article he was writing about commercial real estate. He asked me, "How much do you lease in a year?"

I answered, "Not quite a million."

His response, "New Hampshire only did 800,000 in the entire state."

I responded, "That's why I'm not in New Hampshire. Some deals would escape me. I would need volume."

Those cranes were busy with one project after the other. What a carnival, and I got to be one of the ring masters. All very exciting. Now when I travel I always search for the cranes—we have a special connection. "If you build it, I will lease it" was my mantra.

JOHN A. SOBRATO: THE CONSUMMATE DEALMAKER

Of the Magnificent Seven, John Sobrato was the one who most loved "a deal," though the word deal rang all the developers' bells.

I met him my first year—sports car, license plate which read 'HI DEBT' (which meant he liked leverage—and of course I had no idea what that meant at the time), focused, determined, driven, intimidating, Italian.

It was a couple of years before I actually did a deal with him. Remember, I was working on scraps. Sobrato was working big buildings for large corporations. His inventory contained no scraps. He was going for the gold!

My favorite Sobrato deal story was the 200,000-sq-ft project at Highway 280 and DeAnza that had been occupied by Four Phase. (Coincidentally my husband had worked in that building.) However, Four Phase had moved out and, at that point in time, it was vacant and in search of a tenant.

John had a new company, Apple, that was growing. He had cut a deal with them but the next step was to finance it. No small feat. The insurance company was reluctant, actually emphatic: NO on financing. It was too large a commitment to a one-company use. They wanted multiple tenants to spread the risk. Apple was a young company and that presented a BIG risk. Who knows how long they'd be around? Third objection—it was a technology company, a relatively new segment of the business world. Altogether just too much risk to finance. So he flew back east to meet with the insurance company to get the financing.

This, in itself, was an uncommon event since Silicon Valley rarely acknowledged there were other parts of the world, much less that they had anything that Silicon Valley folks wanted or needed.

This was the perfect platter for John Sobrato, the consummate salesman.

He flew back there to meet with them personally, overcame all the objections, and returned with financing in hand. Today we laugh at the objections, but in the '80s, they were seriously high risks. John was at his best and blew right through them. A grand victory.

For me, the other brilliant business decision Sobrato made was to convince his son to join him. He brought the use of a computer into the organization. His sound principles, ability to listen, his forthright 'one step in front of the other' philosophy brought an amazing strength to the organization. He turned it from a successful entrepreneurial endeavor into a long-lasting corporation that had not only high-tech properties but a huge housing component and an all-present philanthropy arm that still benefits all sorts of the Silicon Valley communities.

Hats off to the Sobrato Organization!

"LOOKING FOR PATTY? FOLLOW THE TRAIL."

THE EARLY BIRD GETS THE WORM

One of the best ways to market a real estate project was to do a personal presentation at the broker's office. I realized that showing up at a broker's meeting was an opportunity to implant my project into the brain of every broker there. I gave great planning to these presentations. One brokerage house was headed by a man named Dennis Chambers, who had been a POW in Vietnam. He ran his office like a military camp. To do a presentation you had to sign up and appear at 7 a.m. I lived forty-five minutes away, and I had to make sure my kids were ready to get to school with a packed lunch.

I was getting one shot, so I dressed in an outfit they would remember. I had a T-shirt that said 'Patience my ass, I'm going to kill something.' And I wore this with flannel bottom pajamas, an ugly robe, worn, pink, fuzzy slippers, and my hair rolled up in big pink curlers to get the full bouffant look. This was before the Barbie phenomenon when everything pink became sacred. I rolled into the office dressed like this. I had brochures in hand and a large poster of the project; I explained the project's benefits and promised to meet them any time to tour.

Dennis was flabbergasted—there we no pink rollers in his platoon.

But I had their attention. Thirty years later this ridiculous attire is still talked about, but I did get their attention, tours, and completed deals. I'm not sure whatever happened to the T-shirt. It was my favorite.

Ah, what a wild way to get scraps for the pile. No one ever tired of crazy outfits at my presentations, and I could always get on any office schedule.

SECURING ONE'S TERRITORY IN THE WILD WEST

In 1986, Cornish & Carey was well on its way to becoming one of the big guns in the Valley, a regional company that had deep relationships that sprang from fifty years in residential real estate. They called it entrepreneurial, but it was really the Wild West. No one had ever had management training, sales training, or much business experience. Some didn't even know Emily Post's book *Etiquette*.

However, there was one solid rule. If you called on a business and the person said they were already working with a Cornish & Carey agent, you were to back off, and say you're in good hands. And, most of the time it worked out. Agents chewed around the edges and sometimes wondered if a woman really counted as a bona fide agent. As a woman, I had to design a way to stake my claim and guard my book of business.

Now, my rules were: 1. Don't look to management to solve a problem. I'd do my own solving. 2. Don't look to management for business. I'd find my own business.

I had two approaches when other office agents tried to poach my clients. The first was gentle and civilized. I'd look them straight in the eye and quietly say, "You can't be serious." Then keep totally quiet while the person would fumble about trying to defend an untenable behavior. A strong stare did the job a good share of the time. But if the deal was larger, they just might try to wrangle their way into the deal or totally dismiss me. Then I had to pull out the big guns.

I am 100% Irish with a hot Irish temperament. I don't see it as a temper. I see it as a means to correct wrongs in the world.

"I have a list." I would say quietly when the agent had tried to step into my deal. "You really want to be on the list?" At first they might not have known about the list but the story spread. For those who didn't know, I'd enlighten them. I'd say, "If the doctor tells me I have six months to live, I'm going to kill you. Now I might die suddenly or get incapacitated and I won't be able to fulfill my list. However, if I do get the six months' notice, you're on the list." Women laughed. Men got terrified. When I went down to the Santa Clara shooting range to learn how to shoot, the list threat got real teeth. "She's serious." Those words spread like wildfire.

I found this an effective way to control the wild beasts from poaching my deals. Soon I rarely had to even explain the list. Everyone knew not to mess with me.

I still periodically get asked about the list from agents. "Do you still have your list?" When an agent asks, I simply say, if the person acted ethically, then no. If not, he's still on the list. The thing is I'm getting older. The chances of me getting a six months' notice are increasing. An agent is far better to go get his own business and not try to get my business. This truth became very clear. The men did leave me alone and rarely was I confronted with infringements. Some are still terrified of me. These must be men of low moral fiber. If you play fair and honorably, you're fine.

My family hates this story. They all say, "There's nothing there to be proud of. It just makes you look mean or weird." None of them are in commercial real estate and I have survived for over forty-four years. I protect and take care of my scraps with a quiet look or a story. It's been very effective.

I don't spend a lot of time complaining about male chauvinism. It doesn't mean I didn't encounter it. It certainly did have its moments. But I choose not to dwell on it, or let it derail me.

"WHAT'S IT LOOK LIKE I'M DOING? I'M WRITING MY CHRISTMAS CARDS!!"

A BEACH HOUSE BONUS

In 1983, an older agent in the Palo Alto office asked me to help him find a building in Cupertino for one of his clients. I think he was a bit intimidated by the young men in the office. A young woman was far more to his liking. However, he had a hard time remembering that I was a woman because he always called me Patrick.

I put a search together and surprisingly found the perfect building in Cupertino, which happened to be across the street from an Apple building. A young developer and an older veterinarian owned the building. We all met and immediately felt comfortable with one another. We agreed on the terms to lease the building. Everything seemed grand. For me, this 60,000-sq-ft building in Cupertino was a fantastic event. I would earn $100,000 on this one deal. I loved this real estate business.

Then the fireworks started. Digital Equipment Corp (DEC) was a big important tech company in the '80s and a formidable competitor to Apple. They were as big as IBM at that time. I did not know that Apple had also met with the developer through a broker from our Palo Alto office the day before. The broker and Apple thought they had the deal for that building. But the young developer had us come in anyway, liked us better, and DEC would pay more rent.

The story goes that an executive from Apple named Steve Jobs and Ken Young of DEC talked on the phone that day and started screaming at each other. Steve Jobs was NOT going to look outside his office window at the DEC sign that would be hanging across the street from him. At the same time, DEC thought this was the best-looking building the company had ever leased. That was the start of one huge argument over the building.

Then supposedly their broker got so angry about losing the deal that he blew up at the developer, went to his home, and the story is that he had a brick of dog poop delivered. Did I mention that we were all young and had no professional rules for our behavior?

I, who had done a large amount of smaller deals, was now right in the ring with the big leagues. Rarely am I quiet, but I really had no idea what to make of any of this.

It turns out DEC was quite willing to pay more for the building and the developer really was not threatened by a woman and an old broker. We got the deal. Since I had not forecasted or ever expected this amazing $100,000 commission, I thought it was Christmas.

Meanwhile, my husband was in a startup company, working an atrocious number of hours. Every time we planned to go away for a weekend, he found a reason to cancel it. Then we got the crazy idea to buy a small second home so that we didn't have to make a reservation. While the thinking was a little faulty, the house became a magical spot for us.

We went over to Santa Cruz one Sunday. Neither of us had ever been there. We ate breakfast and then decided to go look at a few open houses. When we looked at the third house, priced at $125,000 in Aptos with a short walk to the beach, we put in an offer and bought it. We could come whenever we wanted, no reservations. That's how our minds worked. We were young. And this DEC commission was burning a hole in my pocket.

That house, which we still own, even though we now have one further down the road with a view of the ocean, has added a very special dimension to our lives, a special escape from the frantic tempo of Silicon Valley, anytime we want it. The beach still provides that same sense of magic forty-plus years later. We called that house the DEC house. It really had been a totally unexpected miracle.

I invited the developer to use it once as a thank you for such a fabulous deal. He spent the weekend, but he used his time shopping… buying a mobile home park in Aptos. He was a workaholic and made a fortune, but he never had the same kind of good time that we did at the DEC house.

This was a huge scrap for the pile along with a lifetime of wonderful beach time.

THE FALL OF THE WALL

One of my developer clients had a piece of land in Mountain View on Central Expressway, a sterling location. My mission was to get it leased. Getting a tenant for a building not yet built is always challenging. People like to see and walk around what they are committing to. This was early spring and the contractor had 'broken ground.' My sign was the only one up. I was out spreading the word and promising a gorgeous building.

It was a Friday but not just any Friday—it was Good Friday, yes, right before Easter Sunday. Suddenly, I was getting all sorts of calls about the building. However, not the calls I wanted. At 10:30 in the morning, a tilt-up wall had fallen. Everything in the Valley needed to be fast, or so it seemed. These buildings often would be built in less than a year because the demand was so high.

Well, the buildings may get tilted up, but I had the only one where the wall fell! It caused a sensation. Noise, blocked traffic, rumors spread. Why? How? And on Good Friday? This particular developer was not well liked by many of the brokers. He hated to pay commissions—he felt it was a big waste of money and he did not like wasting anything. The stories flew about "the fall."

We did recover. The building did get built and was leased nine months later. The story faded and life moved on.

However, as a good Irish Catholic girl with fourteen years of parochial school with nuns, I still wonder if God himself had spoken. I do believe that when I taught school, I was doing a public service. I educated young minds to make for a better world. But in selling commercial real estate, perhaps I was doing the work of the devil. I was working purely for money. Maybe, I was right... a wall falling on Good Friday!?!

DRESS FOR SUCCESS

One spring day, my work schedule was at a particularly fast pace. I had to be in San Jose at 7:30 a.m. Intel owned and occupied a 150,000-sq-ft building that we were selling.

I had to meet with the CEO, Gordon Moore, to get the paperwork delivered and signed. (This was long before the days of Docusign.) The commute there was forty-five minutes from my home. I got up in the dark, dressed quickly, and drove down there.

My mind was swirling because after that delivery I had to be in West San Jose for a broker open house I was hosting. I did get down to San Jose. Intel had rather unique rules: no offices, just cubicles. Everybody was required to sit in a cube. Silicon Valleyites always danced to the beat of their own drum. Intel believed in no offices and that meant no offices. There was the CEO of Intel in a cube on the open floor.

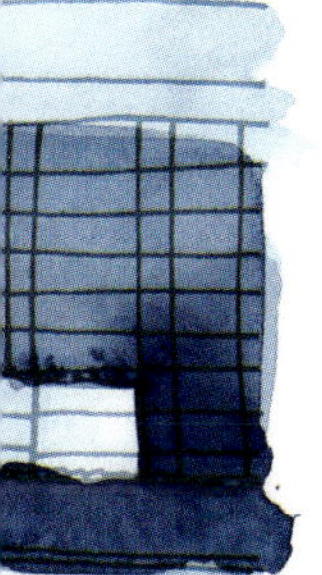

I did find him. He signed the paperwork. Paperwork was so much simpler then. He looked down, then looked up and said to me, "You have two different shoes on."

Indeed I did. I squirmed, "It was dark when I got up this morning. I was thinking about my really busy day. I was wondering how I was going to get everywhere on time. I guess I didn't look down. Sorry." I nodded as if that seemed logical. He thanked me and I was on my way. No cell phones then.

I stopped in the lobby and called home, hoping to catch my husband before he left.

Thank heavens I reached him as he was heading out the door. I asked him to grab a pair of matching shoes, preferably black, and bring them to his office, explaining how that morning I had left with mismatched shoes. He laughed, "How did that happen?"

"Hurrying," I answered. "A busy, diverse day." I took paperwork to the title company. (Incidentally, they did not notice the mismatch.) Then I drove to my husband's office. He'd brought shoes, not the best for the outfit but they were a matching pair. Beggars can't be choosers.

As fast as possible, I headed toward the Greylands project in West San Jose, met the caterer, set up signs, got name tags out—all the chores you need to do when you're hosting 150 brokers at a luncheon to show off a project. Midway through this project luncheon some secretary found me and asked me to come to the phone. Remember, no cell phones yet. Somehow my son had found the phone number where I was. He was calling because he had been in a car accident. I proceeded to give him a full-blown lecture about careful driving... and at the end asked, "Are you all right?" I definitely had the conversation in the wrong order.

That night when I got home I was exhausted. I poured myself a glass of wine. Lesson from the day. Check your shoes. If you start the day with mismatched shoes, the day will just never get on track.

My mantra now is, "All's well, if I have matching shoes on."

"OH, AS IF YOU'VE NEVER DRESSED IN THE DARK."

A CLOSE CALL

In the '80s we received our phone messages on small pink slips that a receptionist wrote down as the calls came in. No voicemail or direct dial yet and we were a busy office. Our receptionist, Kathryn, could not handle much confusion. Such were the makings of a catastrophe.

My eleven-year-old daughter rode her bike to school every day. The trip was only about a mile on safe streets. However, coming home one afternoon she was not paying attention and drove into a parked truck. Neighbors came running out. They called my office and took her to the emergency hospital.

It was now a neighborhood crisis. She had not broken anything but her face looked awful, scraped and bleeding. The hospital tried calling me—no response. Finally, one of the men came home, called the office, and said to Kathryn, "Damn it. Where is Patty? I need to talk to her."

Kathryn told him, "Sir, it's been very busy today and I have this huge pile of pink slips and I just haven't gotten time to sort them yet."

He said, "Well, her daughter is in the hospital and she needs to come home."

Kathryn said, “Yes sir, I’ll go tell her right now.”

At the news, I jumped up, grabbed my keys, ran to the car and drove to the hospital as fast as humanly possible. She was no longer there. I headed home where the neighbors met me. I now felt the equivalent of a witch at the Salem witch trials. I was already considered suspect in the neighborhood. I worked in San Jose, far away. Remember, women were not a big part of the work force then. None of my neighbors worked. I had been divorced AND had kept my own name. I’m certain they were giving thought to calling child services but decided I needed one more chance. I also had the advantage that all these women loved my husband. “How she got him to marry her, I’ll never know,” was often bantered about.

These women stared at me, unforgivingly and unsympathetically. This was what the world was coming to—mothers abandoning wounded children at hospitals until they finished working. Nothing I could say or do was going to change this verdict. The good news that came out of it was that my kids got very special treatment after that. Cookies after school, driven rather than walking to soccer practice, on call for forgotten jackets or lunches.

"SWEETHEART, CAN YOU WAIT UNTIL AFTER MOMMY CLOSES TO BREAK YOUR ARM?"

I was permanently on the “Well, we know those working mothers type” list. Oh well. Life went on. Once inside the house, I examined Diana’s face. It was a mess, but she was okay and all this would go away in a few days. I did give her a bit of a reasonably soft lecture about the need to watch where you were going when you were on your bike or crossing a street.

I do have to say my kids loved that neighborhood, did well in school, and went off to college.

The moving truck came the day Diana graduated. I was off to a new neighborhood.

"I HAVE A CAR PHONE - WHY WOULD I WANT TO GET OUT?"

BELOVED MERCEDES 240D

In my first year in real estate in 1980 I drove a maroon, un-air-conditioned Datsun station wagon. All the marks of motherhood were displayed—jackets, lunch pails, extra shoes, leftovers—imagine the worst. It was all there with a permanent smell of cold Jack-in-the-Box french fries. I needed a new car. Remember, Silicon Valley has a warm climate and add to that my jerky, slam-on-the-brakes driving style. I needed a new air-conditioned car with a trunk.

I fell in love with the Mercedes D—stick shift, windows that rolled up and down manually, the taxis of choice in Europe, sturdy, reliable, a bit of class. It had my name all over it.

I loved driving a stick shift. What else are you doing with your hands and feet? I felt the road driving a stick. Real drivers drove stick shifts, or so I thought.

A couple years later, I added the car phone to the console, and life was heavenly. I felt rich, successful, and so proud of myself.

I honestly never have appreciated cars, but this one I treasured. I figured out how to steer with my knee while drinking soda pop and talking on the phone. Talk about a disaster waiting to happen. I never crashed the car, but the soda pop went all over my clothes more than once. My husband suggested I put barf bags in the back-seat pocket. I actually did have a couple of clients get carsick, but I think they might have been hungover.

I drove that car for twelve years. In 1992, my mother was quite ill and I had little tolerance for much. The car was starting to need a bit of work so I reluctantly traded it in. After all, I had driven it over 250,000 miles. Talk about regret. That car went on to live another 300,000 miles without me.

My husband said, “You’ve gotten as good as you’re going to get with a stick shift. I think it’s time you move to an automatic.” Then I also had to get automatic windows. They didn’t have manual windows in any model but the 240D. That bothered me. Just another thing that could go wrong—and what was wrong with manual windows? You can imagine my protest, later on in life, to keyless cars—utter nonsense.

The men in my office had proclaimed that I needed to send the 240D back to Germany, so the manufacturer could study it. The way I drove was legendary. They said I drove to 50 mph in first gear before I shifted. I don’t think I was that bad, but I might have done that a couple of times.

I remember one day after parking that car, a client asked, “Is that your car?” I nodded. She said, “You didn’t park it. You abandoned it.” I’ve never paid a lot of attention to those lines in a parking lot. No one ever liked parking next to me for fear of how I would exit. I wasn’t as bad as they thought I was, but I certainly wasn’t perfect.

I always knew when gas prices increased. That was the only time the other brokers would drive with me. But after a couple of trips, they thought their lives were worth more than saving gas money and I no longer had to chauffeur them.

A good car is a necessary component to commercial real estate. I've driven Mercedes for forty years and I have Steve Kirksey who has taken care of me these forty years. When I've trashed one, he replaces it. No lectures, no smirks. He just quietly replaces the old one with a new one.

He does tell one great story that I'll share: One Christmas, we took my car in for service. In the display room was another newer Mercedes. Richard said, "When you're ready for another car, that's the next model you should get." He then went and sat in his own car while I arranged for the service.

While I was waiting, I went over to the car in the showroom where there was a salesman who had just started. I said, "I'll take that car."

He said, "But I'm not sure I can get it off the showroom floor for you to drive it."

I said, "I don't need to drive it. I've driven Mercedes for twenty years. I know how they drive."

He then said, "But I don't think I can get it ready for you today."

I replied, "I don't need it today. Talk to Steve. He'll figure out how much of a trade-in I'll get for the one I just dropped off, and I'll write you a check for the difference. I'll pick it up next Monday." He was dumbfounded.

I got into Richard's car to drive us home and said, "Well, that's done."

Richard asked, "What's done?"

I said, "I bought that car, turned the other one in. We'll pick up the new one Monday. Now, let's get to the beach!"

Steve called me later, "I must say you turned the entire car dealership upside down. The salesmen are all in a state of shock. They've never seen a car sale this fast. I'll have the car ready on Monday. Have a good time at the beach."

A SALESMAN'S NEW LIFELINE

In 1984, my life changed dramatically. I purchased a car phone that was installed in my Mercedes 240D. This clunky enormous phone installed in my car console was a very expensive ($1,500 per month) addition.

People talked about heaven, but I had found it. I love to talk and with this new device in my car, I could talk so much more. My commute to the office was three quarters of an hour. Now I added almost two hours to my work day. Two hours of dead driving time turned into two hours of productive time. It was like a miracle.

It was a bit more dangerous for me. I have little respect for cars and did end up in three fender benders while I was talking on the phone. Life became much safer when the hands-free phones became available.

The technology that was happening in the telephone business was mind-boggling. When I was growing up we watched *Space Patrol* on television. Even they did not have car phones.

The tentacles of the technology world were expanding from the domain of the geeks into our everyday lives. Our management used old school economics in running our offices. Any expense took money away from profits. Often our phone system would break down just from the sheer volume of our calls.

Spending money on technology to improve our business was not the first order of the day. Often I sat in the parking lot conducting business because the office phones were down. If the phones were down, I was not a quiet sufferer. Pity the managers that had to deal with me when the phones did not work.

What happened to my day was marvelous, but what it did for the world of communication was exponential. That car phone was the first step toward the miracle—the mobile phone that is in every one's hand today. Email. Cell phone. Google led the digital explosion that changed our lives. Connectivity, information, immediacy were at our fingertips. We were creating the digital age, and the digital age was spreading throughout the world.

I was in the thick of it, loving every minute of it.

"STEP INSIDE MY OFFICE."

GRADUATING TO HIGH-RISES

In 1986, a drastic move… Silicon Valley grew up and breakthrough happened. Santa Clara became the new location for two dramatic, high-rise office buildings, McCandless Towers and Mission Towers. They were only one mile from each other. However, that was their only similarity. McCandless was a premier developer known for its quality and well-thought-out designs. It had successfully built and leased at least six other projects. This was to be the crown jewel complete with a helicopter pad (even though the pad never got used). The building had underground parking, a swimming pool, a full gym and a restaurant. These kinds of amenities were unheard of in 1986.

My friends Leona Hoolahan, Ann Adrian, and I had the assignment to lease it. The project was a delight to work on. It showed well. Everyone was sensible about pricing. It had great views, though I did find the engineers were still a bit unsettled by stacked floors. However, they were warming up to the idea.

Then, later that year, Karim Maskatiya and Sunil Suri built Mission Towers. These two partners were not regulars of the real estate world. This was a different kind of owner/developer. Maskatiya was an entrepreneurial full-fledged character from Pakistan. Suri was an accountant by trade from India. Definitely an odd couple. They had hired three male industrial (not office) brokers from Cornish & Carey—NOTHING happened. This building was the first of what was planned to be four buildings totaling a million sq ft. The tenets of Silicon Valley that Karim Maskatiya knew were different. So, this odd-shaped, triangular building rose up from the ground: unusual ownership, industrial brokers, downdrift in economy. Ingredients for disaster.

Then, to add to the story, Karim's wife was found tied to a chair with a bullet in her head a few years before. Eight weeks later the bookkeeper was found dead in the bay. This struck terror in the male brokers in my office, but for slightly other reasons than you might think.

Long story short, I met Sunil at a real estate event, chatted with him and set up a time to brainstorm with him. No man dared to deal with this building. I decided to try a different path to lease it for him. This was going to be a tough assignment, no doubt about it, but this 250,000-sq-ft building would be the source for a lot of scraps for my pile.

Karim had great people skills—funny, entertaining, and willing to try anything. I liked that, but in real estate to lease the building one has to work every day. That was a foreign concept to him. So he said if he had to come to the office, then he needed to have something good to look at. He called a modeling agency, asked if any of the candidates could answer the phones.

A model named Michelle came to the interview. She fit the bill. Karim said, "If she's here everyday, I'll come in." I thought, "And if she's here every day, I can get the brokers here. The men will come up here to pick up the key from Michelle." This woman was gorgeous and worth her weight in gold. I put aside my feminist philosophy. I needed to get the building leased. I had to move this deal along and I needed Karim in the office everyday. Next move. I needed to break the bad mojo. So I convinced Neiman Marcus to do an old-style fashion show luncheon. I figured that would pull in all the women brokers and the men would be curious. Karim liked this idea. He was warming up to the chaos of the leasing world and the building was gaining a positive image.

We were a team of three women. We argued with the two men, and cajoled and nagged them, but, by god, we started getting deals done. These two owners would fight with one another in a Middle Eastern language. Doesn't everyone's business day flow like this? We all agreed this was the toughest building we'd ever worked on. The triangular shape was particularly challenging. It made for strange layouts. Neither of them claimed the origin of that idea. Then Karim converted the second floor to a retail floor that looked like the red light district in Amsterdam. He had a jewelry store, his barber, a hair salon, and his travel agent. Each suite had red lights around the windows. You get the idea. We just never showed that floor. However, within a year we had the building leased.

My husband was eager to paint my name out of the sign. He kept saying, "We just don't need the money that much that you have to take these kinds of chances."

However, we three women had all gone to parochial schools. For us, this was really funny and interesting. We had leased up the first high-rises in Santa Clara, no small feat. After that, we felt Mount Everest would be easy.

THE SUNNYVALE BLITZ

Silicon Valley was a feast-or-famine daily life. Business life in the tech world reminded me so much of living with a teenage girl. Every day, a crisis with a large dose of drama.

South Bay Development was one of the San Jose developers that were venturing into Sunnyvale. Usually the developer found the land then conceived the product. At this point, he would go shopping for a money partner who could finance it. Then the developer built it and leased it and the developer and money partner shared the profits. In the early days, insurance companies like Copley in Boston were a prime example of this. The plan would be laid out by the developer and insurance company. There would be some contingencies. Because, like with teenage girls, there was always the unexpected.

Technology companies were born, grew, and died quickly. This formula was not like any other industry. It was fast, innovative, creative, and unpredictable. South Bay was at one of those unpredictable moments. These developers did not know Sunnyvale like they knew San Jose.

Moffett Park in north Sunnyvale was a triangular portion of the city, bounded to the west by Moffett Federal Airfield, to the south by Highway 237, and to the east by Caribbean Drive, Baylands Park, and the Twin Creeks Sports Complex. South Bay Development had a new project of 150,000 sq ft that could be divided for tenants of

20,000 sq ft and up. I came up with a scheme—a blitz cold-calling afternoon. I got eight of the executives of South Bay to come out to the project and meet with eight members from our office. We were going to team up with each one of them and now we had eight teams to cold-call all of Moffett. I divided the area into sections. Many of the South Bay owners knew how to cold-call, but not for this much area. Even many of the brokers in my office hadn't made a cold call for a project this large. This was good for all of us. A little bit of basic, straightforward work doesn't hurt anybody. So we went out for an hour walking and talking about the project. Came back, switched partners, and went out again. Trust me, only two hours after, we'd finished up and every company in Moffett Park knew about this project and we had done close to sixty cold calls.

Of course we picked up leads that did not exactly fit the project, but they could go elsewhere. Money is money and a deal is a deal. South Bay was mightily impressed with the ingenuity and hard work we had put into this.

We had beer and food after the blitz. Everybody was quite proud of themselves. We had created a new relationship that would generate other business for all of us. The building did get leased eventually. That afternoon became a solid story of how things got done in the Valley.

Today, Lockheed, Google, Facebook, and Juniper are still very much part of the Moffett landscape. The city of Sunnyvale seeks to add housing and amenities to a flourishing business environment. We did our part. We secured the business element for them.

NED SPIEKER: EMPEROR OF THE OFFICE MARKET

Ned Spieker is the only one of the Magnificent Seven whom I have not personally met. However, I did lots of deals on his office creations. In my early years, I had a circle of properties that I knew how to get to and how to show. Ned Spieker built an office project at Scott and San Tomas. That office of his was in my circle and happened to be one of the first ones he had built.

He had a property manager at the project who would meet me. She'd show the space and I would close the deal. "This is one of the finest office buildings in Santa Clara," would roll out of my mouth. Now, at that time it was the only real office building in Santa Clara that was well designed, well priced, and well run. It worked for me and many of my clients.

Spieker has real estate DNA. He cut his teeth with Trammel Crow and then started his own company in 1987. He was a graduate of UC Berkeley, a real businessman, worked hard, and was well mannered. There were no wild crazy stories about this man. But like all of us we were at the right place at the right time. Ned's reputation as a stalwart businessman served him well in the Valley. He recognized the opportunity, built multiple buildings for the mushrooming tech world, and compiled his fortune.

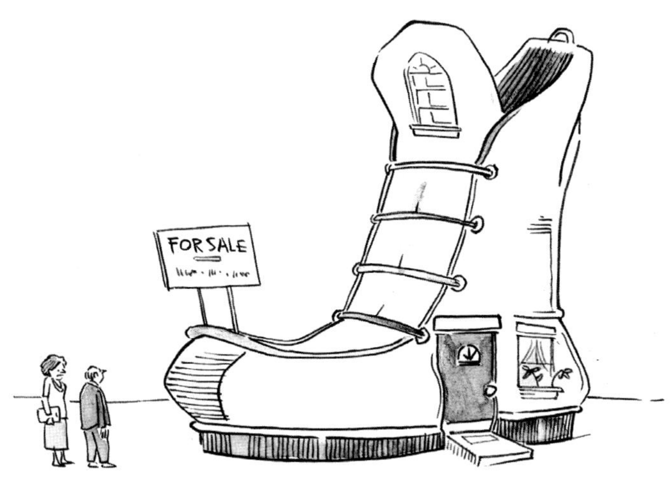

"LET'S LEAVE THIS ONE FOR M^c GUIGAN."

SHACKLETON LEADS THE WAY

In 1994, I contacted Grosvenor Development, one of the largest landowners in London, about a property they owned in Cupertino. Mark, the head of Grosvenor, was the rising star coming from a big real estate success in Hong Kong. With a big success in Cupertino, he'd be running Grosvenor Real Estate's headquarters. I was intrigued with European ownership. This was a very different landlord from my rough-and-ready developers.

So I drove to the Cupertino property, a 50,000-sq-ft building on Results Way. I began to see possibilities. That was always dangerous.

I had just seen a play about Shackleton and found the book *Shackleton's Way* with his rules of leadership. Perfect—I bought seven copies, copied reviews, and highlighted relative facts.

I then drove Kristoff Lodge, my partner on this project, to the Grosvenor office in San Francisco to see the conference room where we would be meeting. We dropped off the books with a professional note, setting the stage for the meeting in a couple of days.

We arrived two days later, ready and on time, and not intimidated by the glorious San Francisco Bay view. We introduced ourselves to Mark and as I did, I commented, "I hope you enjoyed the Shackleton book. We found it inspirational."

Mark smiled, "Every young school lad studies Shackleton." I felt very confident. I knew we had the deal. We played out our performance, how we would lease the building, the process, and our target candidates. We had won the assignment. These kinds of performances are great fun when you know you've already won. At the end I had captain and sailor hats for all, distributed them, and walked out with the assignment. Now to lease it.

The street was named Results Way and Formula One was the sports talk of the day. So I got a big motorcycle, a racing jacket, and two hundred matchbox cars. I laid a track through the building. Brokers had to follow the track to get $50 and lunch. It was a roaring success. We ran out of food and fifty dollar bills, which we ended up delivering the next day. Everyone was in a grand party mood. Mark was gobsmacked by the crowd, the enthusiasm, and the brokers. He was speechless. This kind of party simply did not happen in his aristocratic world. We did deliver a leased building in sixty days. He was elated to go home to London for his promotion.

The next summer I traveled to London, and he invited me to lunch. He toured us through the headquarters bragging about his Silicon Valley experience and gave me an enamel box honoring Grosvenor. He was so appreciative of what I had done.

Then he said, "I have a big project in Liverpool that I'd like you to work on." I told him that he was delightful and I was flattered, but I knew nothing about Liverpool. In fact, I'd never even been there.

His comment: "That's fine. I just want the energy and the enthusiasm." Yes, I was flattered, but I had a family in Silicon Valley. We laughed and I headed home. He stayed in touch.

Liverpool proved to be a bit of a disaster. Mark commented in his note, “I needed the energy and enthusiasm, but you were a pond away.” I wonder if a big Beatles party would have changed the fate of that project?

TWO DAVIDS

Late '90s and Silicon Valley was soaring. The gold rush was on. This period was the pivotal time when the advancement and development of technology led to the innovations that have become integral to our lives today—the web, Google, DVDs, cell phones, seeds of social media.

It was wild and explosive. What a time to be in the real estate business, when all these inventive busy minds needed a building to develop their idea into a company.

Two young men, both named David (Hunter and Russell), arrived in our Santa Clara office thinking this work might be for them. I instantly knew I could have a great time with these two. They were fun-loving, energetic, and curious about the world. Besides our deals, I took them to the museum, biking, and lunch. Great companions, and we laughed and strategized about our deals.

Cornish & Carey had sprung out of a residential company. There were few rules, little supervision, no training. A new hire was given a desk and a phone, told to find someone who needed space, find the space, and get the deal signed.

I think one of the key ingredients of my ability to do this business for decades was my notion of working with another person.

I have great strengths and great weaknesses. I can always find business. I'm terrible at details, but I love talking to people. So I shared almost every deal I ever did. I got to do what I was good at. The others filled in the pieces, and we all made a great deal of money. Each of my two Davids was perfect for these wild deals. I poured the pancake batter. They flipped them and served them.

We had a great mix—youth and experience, a man and a woman team, desire to learn and a desire to teach. In a two-year period, they each made great money, learned the basics of real estate, and decided it wasn't for them. One made over a million dollars, quit, and motorcycled through Australia for a year. He came back, became an architect, left that business, and then went to work in city planning and liked it. I'd rather have my teeth drilled. The other David met a great gal and followed her career to Atlanta where he began working for a senior housing developer.

Interesting that both stayed in the wider world of real estate, but the fire and chaos of commercial real estate did not stick for them. I stayed with my leasing career in the Valley, collecting my scraps, not understanding why they didn't love this crazy world. I began to see this game was not for everybody, but it certainly fit me.

"OH, I'M NOT PLAYING. THIS IS ONE OF THE FEW PLACES I CAN WEAR THESE CLOTHES."

GOLF ANYONE?

Other firms had done events for clients for years but not us. Finally Cornish hired a former Coldwell Banker broker to run the office. He felt we needed to do more traditional outreach activities. A golf tournament where we invited a client for a round of golf was put in place. I signed up. After all, I had golf clubs and played with my husband. To me it was a walk in the park. I never kept score, but I loved the grounds, the clothes, and the tradition of golf.

The day before the event I tried to cancel, but had no luck. Sherry was setting up the event and asked me my handicap. I turned to a fellow and asked, "If you're not a really good golfer, do you have a high or low handicap?" That is a hint of my knowledge of the game. I asked Sherry what was the highest handicap allowed. She called me back after she checked with the golf course. "44," I said, "that's my handicap."

We were put into groups of four and the foursome arrived on the golf course. I was dressed well. I had knickers that I had gotten in Scotland, a jaunty hat and leather golf gloves. I looked the part. One fellow was on his phone the entire time. My client was a real golfer. The other was a beginner. And then there I was. The most you could take on any hole was a 7. I had a lot of 7s. My one exception was that I do not play long par-5 holes. I always need a bit of a break and I believe those holes are reserved for pros. So we moved around the course. I was the only woman that played that day, but I had become used to being the only woman.

When we finished, we headed toward the bar where we all were celebrating our best shot. Chuck got up to announce the winners. His secretary was not versed in golf traditions. Chuck had been busy with getting this first tournament organized. Some details had been overlooked. As he announced the winner, I was #1 with a score of 66.

Chuck was aghast but nothing he could do. Dave Hiebert came in second with a legitimate 68. The laughter set the tone. I accepted my award graciously. I have received many awards in my career but this statue sits in the front.

The next day I wrote a circular to the office that I would be delighted to take any of them shopping for better golf clothes. If one dressed well, one played well. No one signed up. I've never played in a tournament again. When you begin at the top, the only way to go is down.

AN ENGLISH GENTLEMAN

Among all the thousands of cold calls I've ever made, the sales gods did provide me with one very special client—an amazingly highly-educated English gentleman, Tony Ley.

His background was so different from the young bold entrepreneurs I was used to dealing with. He was a voice of reason, worked consistently, never lost his cool, listened to his employees, never was daunted by challenges of starting and growing a business. There were few men like him.

His background was steeped in the Slumberger tech world, an enormous tech company in France. He had run research facilities in Paris and Palo Alto. He arrived in the Valley and felt the vibe. This was a spot where technology was exploding with revolutionary ideas. He found a group of engineers and began to form a company. That company was originally called Harmonic Lightwave, which provides a range of products and solutions that enable satellite, wireless, fiber, and cable television companies to offer interactive services.

Tony held an MA from Cambridge, an SM from MIT, was a fellow of the IET, an honorary fellow of the SCTE (UK), a senior member of IEEE, served as a trustee for the Center for Integrated Systems at Stanford as a member of the advisory board at the Materials Processing Center at MIT, and is named as an inventor on twenty-eight patents. This kind of resume was not to be found anywhere in Silicon Valley. Add common sense and level-headed decision-making to the mix, and he was a talented man indeed.

He was a proper Englishman. He had a Scotsman for his CFO and an Irishwoman, me, as his real estate agent. This was an unbeatable trio. When we went into meetings, our presentation was exceptional. People paid attention, and by and large, we got what we needed.

I leased his first facility in 1988 and we did fourteen more transactions until his retirement. His values, work ethic, and foresight in business were unparalleled. His CFO kept the ship steady and moving forward, and I, his wild Irish lass, made sure real estate happened timely and on budget.

My most outstanding contribution was his clean room. In 1994, he needed a clean room built to move the product forward. A clean room is a specially built room with large amounts of electricity and HVAC to provide a "clean" environment to build and test a product. The price to build this particular one for Harmonic Lightwave was $400,000, an enormous sum in 1994. We found the right building, but we needed the clean room built in it. The cost was challenging. The property was a sublease which meant that the company responsible to the landlord was still responsible for the rent even though the company was no longer occupying the building.

The market was at a low dip and the landlord needed a tenant in the building. We were a possibility.

Tony's marvelous English presence in this whirling dervish tech world lent a touch of sanity to our prospective landlords. I had somehow wrangled a meeting of the two principles. We convinced them of the value of Harmonic Lightwave and the need to build this specialized room. I convinced the landlord to pay up front for the cost of the clean room. I have to admit this was not just unusual. It was an Irish miracle, but we got it to happen.

We walked out of that meeting acting as though if they didn't do this for us, we had three other owners that would. Brazenness at its best!

The company executives convened and agreed. We got that contract signed in no time and Harmonic was off to the races. That exciting moment came on October 3, 1996. The event to celebrate that day was one big company party. We had all the folks involved. The mayor was there. The VCs, the employees, the key customers, all in this newly refurbished building.

This was a major coup and put them on the road to going public. Being involved in a company going public was like a wedding, college graduation, and birth of your first child all rolled into one. I got to be in the front row with Harmonic for this monumental event.

When Tony gave his speech, he gave me a shout-out honoring me for my work in getting the right facility at the right time. I was so honored I still remember that event thirty years later. This kind of involvement and appreciation could only happen in such an innovative, explosive time.

I found it amazing what I could accomplish once I put my mind to it. This was beyond rewarding, but I did notice that the pile was growing and some of those scraps were really solid real estate transactions. Real money, far more than teaching school could ever yield. I still smile when I think people were paying me to do this. It was astonishing. I loved these deals.

"I MISS THE OLD WAY OF COLD-CALLING."

STRIKE UP THE BAND

In the late '80s, McCandless had designed and built a cutting edge, versatile park with eleven buildings. A place for young companies to grow and expand in one area. The concept was flawless. The location was in Milpitas, which was coming into its own. Everything was right except the market. It had turned sour.

I have often said that Silicon Valley was an area gone bipolar. It was boom or bust. This project was bought, designed, and built when the Valley was booming and it arrived ready for tenants as the bust hit.

We had eleven buildings and an entire street to lease. The investor was from Southern California and was skeptical of technology on a good day. These were not good days.

I remember picking him up at the airport, opening my trunk to put his suitcase in. He started lecturing me about the state of my trunk. Remember, I have two kids and the trunk held the residue of their lives—old sandwiches, shoes, dirty clothes from practice—a real mess.

This fellow proceeded to give me a quality lecture about the value of a clean trunk. I was just thankful I was no longer driving a station wagon. I am not the beacon of detail. This fellow was the maestro of minutiae. This was going to be a fun afternoon.

So, as usual in a downturn, we needed activity. My reputation for throwing great broker parties was spreading. These were a lot of buildings totaling over 250,000 sq ft. We needed a lot of brokers.

The buildings were spread out—too far to walk and too short to drive to. Solution: a six-person golf cart.

Next was the broker party. I had to get them all to the project. Most of the men in Silicon Valley loved sports and Stanford. Stanford had this zany, totally ragtag, nonconforming band. They prided themselves on their craziness. They would be perfect. I called the athletic department, tracked down the band director and asked if they would perform at a one hundred-person lunch in Milpitas. I offered $1,000 and a keg of beer. We were on.

The promise of the Stanford band got the brokers out. We had a typical game day lunch, hats with our project name on them, lots of game paraphernalia. The party began. The band marched down the street. The crowd followed—picking up chips, ice cream, hot dogs as they danced and hollered… Wildly successful.

My Los Angeles investor flew up for the event. He was in a state of shock. How would this do any good? Disorganized Stanford band, jumping around like banshees. Hot dogs and ice cream for lunch. Golf carts running up and down the street. He wanted CEOs going through buildings.

I explained to him this was the first step: break into the company with a broker talking about the project. He was skeptical. Promptly we got tours. We met many nonqualified tenants, but at least people were touring. Our rent was 50 cents a sq ft. Our operating cost was

80 cents a sq ft. Rent was not the issue. Credit and simple build-out was our criteria. Money would be made on the renewals.

We did it. We filled Milpitas and actually had only a few bankruptcies; it was a constant coming and going and we had some laughs at the array of potential tenants that did tour.

Incidentally the band loved it too. They'd actually made money being crazy. The investor made delayed money—it just took time. In future visits, he no longer asked for me to pick him up. He rented his own car when he came up to check the project—no dirty trunk for him.

"I THINK HE'S REALLY ENJOYING THE PERSONAL TOUR."

SETTING BOUNDARIES

As the years rolled along, we did add a few more agents to the office roster. Even then, the atmosphere in the office was still that of a rowdy sales office in an entrepreneurial environment with few rules. We were young with burgeoning technology all around us, lots of opportunity, and amazing job growth. We could feel the heartbeat of real estate. Life was fast and we were making deals.

One afternoon a baseball flew across the office and hit me hard in the face. I blew up and left the office. The boys had crossed the line and my Irish temper exploded. Fortunately, I only had a swollen side of my face and no lasting damage, but enough was enough.

I went into the manager's office for some other business question when I mentioned the baseball incident. He proceeded to say, "Well, Judy, you dish it out with the best of them." He had been the manager for two years. I had been a top performer, given the Hall of Fame award, and was now hit by a baseball. And he didn't even know my name.

I quietly said, "You really need to know a bit more about me. Pull out your calendar. We need to have lunch." He did not dare to refuse.

I took him to the Lion & Compass, one of the nicer go-to restaurants close by. As we chatted, I noticed that my best client ever was at a nearby table, Tony Ley, the CEO of Harmonic Lightwave. Remember Tony, the English gentleman? I introduced them and Tony went, "Do you know how fabulous she is? She handles all our real estate. She managed to get our clean room built for us, and managed all our real estate moves with skill and thoroughness, and that all on time and on budget. Patty is fantastic."

My manager then said, "Didn't that company just go public a couple months ago?" I answered, "Yes, and I got a marvelous shout-out at the IPO party, a big event." I had not known Tony would be there that day, but the lunch could not have been better timed to make my persona known.

When we left, my car was right out front. I went to the restaurant often. So I knew the parking valet well. He'd always park my car by the door. When we came out, he smiled and handed me my keys. My manager said, "He really likes you. You must tip him well."

I quietly turned to him, "Yes, I tip him well, because he does a great job. But he also likes me, because I remember his name."

As we drove back, he asked, "So, where are you going this summer?" I said, "London."

"Have you ever been there before?" he queried. "Often," I responded. He asked, "How many times?" I answered, "Well, about twenty-five."

I thought he'd fall out the door. He said, "You go to London like I go to Lake Shasta." I replied, "I've gone once to Lake Shasta."

Then I continued, "I was an English major. I taught school for years.

I really like Europe, and I always start in London. You and I live in different worlds, but we can still know and respect each other."

He thanked me for lunch, and, to his credit, after that day, he was always respectful, thoughtful, and appreciative. Meanwhile, I had set a tone for business behavior at work. Throwing things in the office was banished. We had new boundaries. The young man who had thrown the ball quit a few months later. I had managed my temper. Success for everyone.

LEASING THE CROWN JEWEL

McCandless' new project in Santa Clara was San Tomas, a four-building, two-story complex located on San Tomas and Central Expressway. I was really excited to promote this project. It was flawless. Then I found out that two of the managers and another broker from my office had gone directly to Birk seeking the exclusive.

My rule was, and has always been, not to go to a manager to solve a problem, but to solve it. I did not go to management looking for business. I found my own business. It would not have done any good to go to these three men.

I called Birk McCandless and Steve Sund, Birk's lieutenant, to take them to lunch. After all, they were the decision-makers. As far as I could see, the brokers were not going to be sympathetic to me, so I didn't ask. I had to convince Birk, the owner of McCandless, myself. We chatted about how well his past projects had leased. Then I said, "I understand three men in our office would like the new San Tomas project. You have just gotten a new house in Tahoe. Imagine if you went home to your wife saying to her, 'Mary, I have this new house. I know you are so busy with these three girls and keeping our home in order that I've gotten someone just like you to take care of the Tahoe house.'"

I added, "I think Mary would be rather upset about that decision. I'm not sure it would help your relationship. I feel the same way about San Tomas. I've worked hard, done a great job for you, and I think I've earned the right to that business. Now your success is the most important matter. I promise you. And if I falter or get overwhelmed, I will immediately resign and you can put another team on it. But I do feel strongly that I have earned the first right to the business."

The rest of the lunch we talked about the market and my strategy for leading the project. As we got up to leave, Birk said, "I've got to hand it to you. I came to lunch as a courtesy for work well done with no intention of changing my mind. Your point is a fair one. You have the business."

We started to market and tour the project and of course planned a big broker barbecue. I had Steve with two of the Cornish owners barbecuing hot dogs and hamburgers. Because it was summer, I had my thirteen-year-old daughter available to help. So she was assigned the job of walking brokers through the project. I told her what to say and to make sure they saw everything. Then she should collect a card and give them a bottle of wine. We finished up. Everyone was in great spirits, feeling the event was a big success.

I noticed my daughter had two stacks of broker cards. I asked, "Why two?"

"One stack is the cute brokers. The other stack, not-so-good-looking." I thought about it. It was as good a way as any to divide the gang.

She said, "You know I could do this business."

I answered, "Yes, you could, but you have high school and college before you can even think about it."

We hit pay dirt with this project quickly. Intel was "in the hood" and needed space immediately. "How fast could you deliver the ready-to-move-in project?" they wanted to know. Timing was very important to them, and they put a deadline on us with heavy daily penalties.

At that time, HVAC units were in short supply. John Arrillaga, another major developer, always a wily old fox, somehow knew the shortage of HVACs and had bought a warehouse of them. He said to Intel, "If you're in a hurry, come to me. I can deliver." He was our competition. But we wrangled the deal away from John, and now had to deliver. We went on a hunt and found the necessary HVACs. We figured out our construction time. With two weekends of overtime, we could do it. You have no idea how many donuts in the morning and ice cream in the afternoon I delivered to those workmen. A smiling face and food—does it every time. We made our deadline.

The irony, after all the frantic work, was that Intel had forgotten to order the phones. So they were delayed three weeks.

I ended up just continuing on my real estate path collecting my scraps. My daughter never followed in my footsteps. She didn't like scraps. She went right for the gold.

CARL BERG: LARGER THAN LIFE

One of the few Magnificent Seven who was not a native Californian, Carl Berg was born in New Mexico and received his BA from University of NM.

He began his career in Texas with a mortgage company before making his way to California, where he partnered with John Sobrato. Both in their twenties at the time, the two launched Midtown Realty, focusing on selling single-family homes, with guidance from John's mother, Ann Sobrato.

In 1979 they each went their own way. Carl headed south to San Jose where he would build large campuses for high-tech companies. John Sobrato set up his operation in Cupertino and focused on R & D buildings.

Carl invested in his companies, PGE plants, and golf courses throughout California. His investments were far broader and more diverse than the ones of the other Magnificent Seven.

When I say Carl was larger than life, it has a special meaning for Carl. He was enormous, close to 400 lbs at times in his life, but always healthy. And he organized his paperwork by "borrowing shopping carts from the neighborhood grocery store." Doing a deal with him was entering into a no-rules, Star Wars-type bar. He'd turn to the client about a legal comment and say, "I'm not going to do that," whatever it was, then he'd cross out the passage.

I once did a 13-million-dollar transaction in three days with him involved. I have been accused of having only one speed but Carl beat me. One of my partners on one of the deals kept saying, "We're going to end up in jail." I'd just keep going. My retort: "Don't worry—I have some great black-and-white clothes," and we'd get a good laugh and get the deal done.

Carl did not spend much personal money, but he loved a deal where he could spot a profit. He was unique and intuitive, a force to be reckoned with, and a delightful, full-fledged character.

DOT-COM BIZARRE

In 1999, the speed, the craziness and the tech world's "can-do-no-wrong" attitude was at its peak. I could feel this wildness was just not sustainable. Trouble was coming. I was right. A couple of my deals were too bizarre, I could feel us going over the edge.

My brother had given me a lead to a new venture capitalist. I met with him and the CEO he had chosen to run this newly funded company. I talked with them. They wanted a building that day in North San Jose or Fremont, 15,000 to 20,000 sq ft. I said give me a couple of hours to put together a tour and secure keys, and I'll be back at noon to share possibilities.

A tour. One of my tenets is, "You never lease a building with one tour." This day proved me wrong.

We toured six buildings. They chose one. I called the developer and gave him the terms of the deal so he could fill in the blanks on the lease. I told him I'd bring financials and a business plan to his office by 3:30. I needed the lease to get it signed. I picked up the lease, drove back to the VC's office where the two were waiting for me. The CEO signed a five-year lease at asking rent that would start in two weeks. I had completed a 17,000-sq-ft, five-year deal in one day that resulted in a $45,000 commission to me. I have to call this more than a scrap—it was one huge comforter on my pile.

I drove home feeling like I had just won the Indy 500. This simply defied common sense but you had to grab the deals while you could. No one could duplicate that day.

Another out-of-body experience is the wild dot-com deal that was a 20,000-sq-ft building in Mountain View that Carl Berg owned. There was and will only be one Carl Berg ever in the universe, only one of the Magnificent Seven developers that built the buildings in Santa Clara aka Silicon Valley. Carl lived in his own world, he did what he wanted, lived where he wanted, invested in what he wanted: PG&E power plants, golf courses, Silicon Valley buildings, cures for cancer. He was one eclectic man, a big boy, all 400 pounds of him, and he loved chocolate. That was my secret weapon with him, which made all my deals go down quite easily.

In the beginning of Silicon Valley tech development, John Sobrato and Carl Berg had been partners. They split the partnership in the late '70s quite amicably. This Mountain View building ended up in Carl's portfolio. He prided himself that he had built this building in less than a year for $16 a sq ft. The price was unbelievably cheap even in the '70s when it had been built. Carl was frugal. He really hated to spend money on tenant improvements. So everything he leased was as is. That was his rule.

His new tenant for this Mountain View building was a young bright English engineer running a tech company who knew nothing at all about how to outfit a building so it could be used as an office. He'd hired a CFO from Southern California that had worked for Disney.

This fellow was in charge of the build-out. The requirements were basic: a dozen offices, five conference rooms, kitchen, lab area. He decided to add character to this floor plan. He was neither an engineer nor an architect nor a designer. He decided to build the doors of the offices "Disney" style. No one even looked at what he was doing. When it was finished it looked like Alice in Wonderland worked there. Every door was of uneven shape (requiring very expensive unique cutting and building). Colors were Disneyesque, certainly imaginative and creative, but NOT Silicon Valley style.

The president groaned but worked with the crazy design. He needed to get a product out. He was in a race to take the company public. I was in a state of shock when I saw it for the first time, but I dared not say anything.

When the dot-com collapse happened about eighteen months later, the company collapsed like so many others. Carl actually came out to see the building for the first time. He almost exploded. Carl had never been to Disneyland. So he had no idea what the origin of the design was. He got a contractor out immediately and actually tore out walls. A new phenomenon for him. He knew no one was going to lease this space as is. The CFO returned to Southern California. He just could not meld with Silicon Valley thinking and I personally thought Disneyland was far more his cup of tea.

These two deals are just two of my crazy dot-com deals. No wonder there was a collapse. There was a flood of venture capital money, buildings mushrooming up everywhere, companies going public steadily, tech stock prices skyrocketing, and then suddenly it blew up in 2000. A huge mess was created. I'm not sure if we'd all learned a lesson or we were all just getting older, but business after that downturn became a bit more rational.

However, there remained a steady stream of bright engineers, venture capital, a market that was definitely using technology at an ever-increasing rate. New ideas and business growth started back up but at a saner pace. I think.

DAVID J. BROWN: THE NEW SHERIFF IN TOWN

Dave was yet another California-born developer who saw a dream and made it happen.

Dave came into development more traditionally than the other Silicon Valley developers. He was well educated and got a job working for Boise Cascade to develop the southern part of Silicon Valley-San Jose. Dave sensed amazing possibilities there. He cut a land deal with Boise Cascade for 50 cents a sq ft with borrowed money, and then he was off and running. San Jose was to become a big sky country under Dave Brown's direction.

In the '70s, most of the commercial development was all north of San Jose. The San Jose residential development was exploding but the city needed to build a commercial component. The land that formed the San Jose airport, the 101, and the 17 was a triangular piece of land called Orchard Properties—the Golden Triangle—which became Dave's Legoland.

In his formidable years, he gathered contractors, bankers, developers, and brokers who were the weavers of his empire. His financial tool was to joint venture with New England Life Insurance to design, construct, and lease the buildings. With his team he eventually built a million sq ft a year.

Dave made an indelible mark on the southern part of Silicon Valley and an integral part of the lore. He had a definite Western style. I always felt I was in a bit of the Old West when I was working in the Orchard world. There were lots of "cowboys" in that operation.

After the first tour, the story of my driving became notorious because Dave Brown had gotten carsick with all of my jerky starts and stops. Thus, on the second tour the fellows insisted on driving motorcycles to avoid getting in my car. So Leona and I climbed on the back of the bikes. I must say the Orchard style of dealmaking was a bit different.

The term the Wild West is often used to describe the early days of Silicon Valley.

Orchard Properties wore the Wild West title well.

HI! GOD SUGGESTED I GIVE YOU A CALL ABOUT ONE of HIS PROPERTIES...
Professional Name-Dropping

HITTING THE FIREWALL

It was late 2000 and the Valley was bustling. Venture capital was gushing. Tech companies that had gone public were soaring. There was a shortage of space. The Valley felt invincible. People kept saying, "This is different from the other economic downturns, because we have diversified." Now that idea shows you how little we really knew about economics. We must have missed the chapter about supply and demand. We were so caught up with ourselves, we thought diversified meant several tech products. Tech had infiltrated into all sorts of different industries. We were recession proof. Right? Wrong.

Cisco was the big boy in the tech world at that time, growing exponentially. Everyone needed a router. It serves two primary functions: managing traffic between these networks by forwarding data packets to their intended IP addresses and allowing multiple devices to use the same internet connection.

Every company that had a computer needed routers. What no one paid attention to was that there were companies that were resellers. They bought routers and resold them. All was well until it wasn't. When there was a slowdown, Cisco was in effect competing with itself. The avalanche started.

In the Valley there was never a slowdown. It was on or off, boom or bust. The bust was starting and almost overnight the phone in the office stopped ringing. Our manager actually called the phone company thinking the lines had been cut. It was an eerie silence.

I had represented a large 50,000-sq-ft building in a marginal location when the market hit the wall. The owner, whose name shall remain unknown, lived in Denver and was the western manager for a national real estate investing company. We had worked far too long on the deal. He wanted an additional 25 cents/sq ft in rent. Cisco, who had been unstoppable, was suddenly stoppable and pulled the letter of intent, canceling our deal. There was no going back. Cisco did not need any more real estate at any price.

My client called. He could not believe it. He lived in Denver and had heard about the speed and need of the Valley but had never experienced a Silicon Valley downturn and this was a big one. Naturally he started questioning me, then lecturing me. His rant went on and on and on. I put him on speaker phone and started addressing my Christmas cards. No reason to waste precious time. He was just going to have to wear himself out and all for an extra quarter. Now he'd lost not only the quarter but the original dollar and this building was going to sit empty for a very long time. An empty building is worthless to a real estate investment company. Finally the crescendo hit. He said, "And I am holding you personally responsible for this travesty. You caused this dot-com bust!"

I couldn't help but laugh. I do admit I'm no shrinking violet but this was real power he was endowing me with, causing the dot-com bust. Well, I said, "Please don't tell my husband. He'll cut up all my credit cards." Even he laughed, but he still was not happy.

Our mantra became "Stay alive till 2005." Between March 2000 and October 2002, the NASDAQ fell from 5,048 to 1,139, erasing nearly all of its gains during the dot-com bust. By the end of 2001, most publicly traded dot-com companies had failed.

The real estate world was turned upside down. In good times, we were like obstetricians delivering darling babies. In the downturns, we were like cancer doctors delivering morphine to lessen the pain. The deals and the company stories were in a dreadful state. No one was happy. Was technology over? Would we ever dig ourselves out of this hole?

Of course we did. Buildings were sold for redevelopment. Venture money returned to feed young companies. New tech ideas started sprouting up. Indeed we were up and running, a bit more subdued, but ready again to change the world. My Colorado client's company decided to switch into the management of apartments, a much more stable kind of investment. He could understand that kind of business better.

I still get a Christmas card from him every year. At one point he does admit, "I'll never figure out how those folks think." He's not alone. Tech is its own form of crazy. It moves so quickly. People still have little fear of failure. I've often felt the term "on the spectrum" was specifically invented to describe Silicon Valley. A unique place for people who are hyperfocused on one thing or one skill in a space of rarified air where your ideas can become reality and you can actually change the world.

My credit cards were back working.

PIZZAS ARE ON THE WAY

Part of the aftermath to the dot-com fiasco was that a number of buildings got new ownership. The phrase "back to the bank" was a common one as many developers were no longer able to finance the project. So the building was returned to the lender. This became a regular occurrence in the dot-com bust. An entire new breed of ownership for real estate agents to work with—the lenders. These "owners" of the building were not tech-savvy, did not believe in Silicon magic, nor had any building experience. This was the East Coast financial world—wanting the money out and the project off the books. No nonsense, none of the Silicon Valley fairy tales. This owner was more interested in getting rid of a project that was costing money than making any.

Somehow Frank Cox, Phil Trautman, and I landed the exclusive with this big New York investment house which was responsible to get a tenant for a 50,000-sq-ft, single-story building, the traditional R & D that had been the darling of the Valley. However, at this point in time, there were dozens of them. We had to differentiate this one that was a bit buried on a small street. There was nothing special or unique about it. So we had to create a story and get a tenant.

Obviously a broker lunch was immediately planned. If you can get a broker to find the building and walk through it, it gets in the human computer called the brain of the broker. When they meet a client who is remotely interested in a building in that size and location, it hopefully pops up and you get a tour, which ultimately may lead to a deal. That's the hope, at least.

We decided beer and pizza would be an ideal fit for this rather nondescript building. It seemed like a beer-and-pizza kind of building. It could work for most companies, but nothing special to rave about it. These buildings were assigned to middle managers in these investment banking companies. Their mission was to get rid of it as fast as possible and spend as little money as possible. This was not a relationship-building opportunity. This was transactional. We knew the assignments. We were hired guns. Get rid of it.

Phil, Frank, and I were a great team. We had a great time and we got things done. We knew all the brokers, and each brought a different skill in working together. My skill was to get a luncheon set up: invitations out and calls to get folks there. We had the New York team coming. This was so out of their wheelhouse of dealmaking that it was great fun to get them involved until… the big screwup.

When the food did not show up, I called the caterer. I had given the wrong day. This, sadly, was pretty typical of me, flying around doing all sorts of deals in different areas. Mistakes did happen. This one was a doozy. We three were there with New Yorkers. I had decorations and tables, but as morning crept along—still no food.

Men to the rescue. Phil immediately called the local pizza parlor and somehow got thirty pizzas that he picked up in short order. Frank went to the store and loaded up on drinks.

Miraculously, by 12:15 we had food and drinks. Nothing was pretty, but there were napkins and plates. Disaster avoided! Phew! Brokers are like teenage boys—as long as food was there, they walked the building, met the lender, and got back to work. I honestly don't think they even realized what an almost disaster it could have been. I invited our New Yorkers for later that evening to my house to watch the NCAA tournament basketball games and served a proper dinner.

We had all survived. They were really great folks. We all laughed about it. We did lease the building and I filed in my brain three ways to make sure I get the RIGHT date in the future. Even though I still periodically miscalculate a date. None quite as big as this one. This indeed was a scrap, a bit tattered and odd-shaped, but still went on the pile.

"YOU AIM HIGH, McGUIGAN. WE LIKE THAT IN A REALTOR."

SUNNYVALE VERSUS GENEVA

In June of 2000, the market was in the dot-com bust cycle. It was not only slow but a bit grueling. I had the exclusive on a 150,000sq ft building on Geneva Drive in Sunnyvale. Every building has its challenges and this one was no exception. American Hospital Supply had the Koll Company, with New England Life Insurance as its financial partner, build a building especially for their needs. This kind of real estate is called a "build to suit." It's a great deal for developers because the lease-up risk goes away... until the tenant moves out. Then you have the equivalent of a custom-made suit that really doesn't fit anybody.

This gem was a tough sell but as always the location was in our favor. Network Appliance was at the time a high roller and our building was well located for them. We put it in escrow. The deal fell deadly silent and, as I suspected, they had dropped it. As it happened, I was on my way to Switzerland. There'd be no deal, but I'd deal with it when I returned. This was an unusual trip offered by a therapist who lived in Santa Cruz and led these highly affordable two-week hiking trips to Switzerland.

Switzerland is beautiful. Hiking is walking. The price was amazingly low. What could be better? I signed my husband and me up. As it turned out, lots of things could have been better. This therapist found remote, dull villages that were cheap because there was absolutely nothing to see or do there. The restaurants had boring simple selections. We took buses to go to trails so we could climb on rocks, over streams, always careful of not falling while he'd tell stories of injuries and even a death on one of his trips. He got his jollies by making us race to trains. We'd have seven minutes to get to the station. Fourteen days of this was not my idea of a good time.

In 2000, there were no cell phones and these villages had very little public communication. At one village, I waited forty-five minutes in line to use the only pay phone in the place. Those were also the days you dialed an international number, then your phone number, then your code, then the number you were dialing. Grueling. Richard and I had talked about me slowing down or even retiring. This vacation proved to me that was not going to happen any time soon. I was missing my crazy wonderful people-filled days.

The Swiss women swept their porches and stacked the fire wood perfectly neatly. The wood stack looked like match boxes. However, I discovered the suicide rate in Switzerland was surprisingly high. There was nothing to do. Swiss wine was not my favorite. These were definitely not my people.

On our way home, we stayed the last night in a real hotel in Geneva, Switzerland. Hallelujah! I could retrieve my messages, at last. Carl Berg had called me. "Do you still have that piece of crap on Geneva in Sunnyvale?" Carl had no filter and led a "Carl-directed" life.

I sadly answered, "Yes," and added that I'd be home to ramp up to lease or sell it.

"Well, if you can get them to agree to 15 million, I'll buy it. I'm coming out of a trade on another property, but I need to close it in six days."

"No problem, I'll be in your office tomorrow and I'll get this deal done." Ah, did this feel good. Back to chaos, work, and crazies.

I am not the beacon of paperwork. So, to get a copy of the contract, I had to go to the attorney for Network Appliance. I told him my office demanded a copy of the contract or I would lose my license. That was a lie. Then I went to the Good Earth Bakery to pick up a dozen peanut butter cookies. Carl loved these cookies. I rolled into his office with cookies and a contract in hand. We took a bottle of Wite-Out to that same contract, changed the date, the price, and the buyer.

I called the title company agent to come down and tell Carl about the building. We did not have time to pull a recent report. Carl said that the insurance company was afraid of their own shadow. "They've checked and rechecked. I'm fine. Besides, if something outrageous was overlooked, I'll sue them." I thought hmmm… that makes sense.

The next step was getting the sellers to sign. The Koll Company was headquartered in Orange County, and even if I couldn't recall the CEO's name, I knew his secretary and that he loved golf. I found her, and said, "I know he's playing golf, but he wants this deal. You don't want to be responsible for getting in his way."

I called the golf club, said to whoever had answered that this had to be signed and that he requested these papers immediately. I faxed the contract to the golf course, had a person take a cart to the hole he was playing, and believe it or not, he signed it. It was his own approved contract. Only the price, closing date, and buyer were different and he really wanted to get this building off the books.

The whole deal was so unconventional and bizarre, but it got rid of this eyesore.

I was still jet-lagged, really exhausted, but by heavens I had done it! The world was simple and straightforward. And I was not in Switzerland.

A few months later a fast-rising company, Global Crossings, was desperate for a big building with a lot of power. This building was not pretty but it was loaded with power and they bought it for $45 million. Carl loved that story. "I made $30 million and only had to put my hand in my pocket to pull out a cookie."

I still shiver when I think of these deals with Carl. It's a miracle that I didn't end up in prison. Cities, permits, lawyers, financing were all so different. However, every time I wear black and white I think, "I could have worn this in prison."

" OTHER THAN THE MOUNTAINS, AND THE CHOCOLATE, AND THE BEAUTY, AND THE WINE, AND THE HIKING, AND THE VIEW, WHAT IS THERE TO DO IN SWITZERLAND?"

JIM MAIR: CONSTRUCTION PAVED HIS WAY TO GOLD

Jim discovered California in college. He came to Silicon Valley to build his career, did only one job interview with Grubb & Ellis, and was hired. Real estate became his focus. That career decision took him from being a broker to the Hall of Fame for South Bay developers—one of the Magnificent Seven.

Interestingly, Dave Brown, one of the other men in that Hall of Fame, hired Jim as his broker to develop Foster City. Through that position, Jim discovered the Silicon Valley formula—buy a piece of land, lease it, finance and buy another piece.

Jim chose a different path from the other Magnificent Seven. In 1978, he started South Bay Construction which broadened the core of his business. He used his capital to build a team of people. In most cases he chose to buy, build, then sell. He structured his business with people. There were about twenty folks involved with South Bay Construction.

It is not by chance that he is the only one whose name is not in the name of his company. Jim built his business with partners and with construction. He built a company, not an empire. But Jim was a highly approachable leader who recognized talent, partnered with all sorts of talent, and liked making deals.

His main backyard was San Jose and environs. In that territory, South Bay not only built commercial buildings of all uses and sizes, but with his strong construction team he also built for other real estate companies, partnered with insurance companies, repositioned property, and added value by reconstruction. Jim built medical buildings, manufacturing plants, and industrial parks. He must have touched over 36 million sq ft of real estate over the course of his career.

Today, South Bay Construction remains a mainstay of the commercial real estate world in Silicon Valley.

Accolades, Jim!

PUTTING MOUNTAIN VIEW ON THE MAP

In the fall of 2003, Silicon Valley was still a bit reeling from the dot-com fiasco. Mountain View had this enormous Shoreline Business Park that was languishing. A consultant friend of mine, Leigh Boyd suggested to Ellis Berns, the economic development director, that he call me to brainstorm some way to create some activity in the area. Ellis had brilliantly devised the plan where the city of Mountain View would lease rather than sell the land that the city owned in the park to create a steady income for the city. They really wanted this park to be successful. A variety of entrepreneurial developers also owned large sections of the park. The idea behind it was that this park could be another Stanford Research Park. Certainly a lofty ambition. Little did they know how successful it would become.

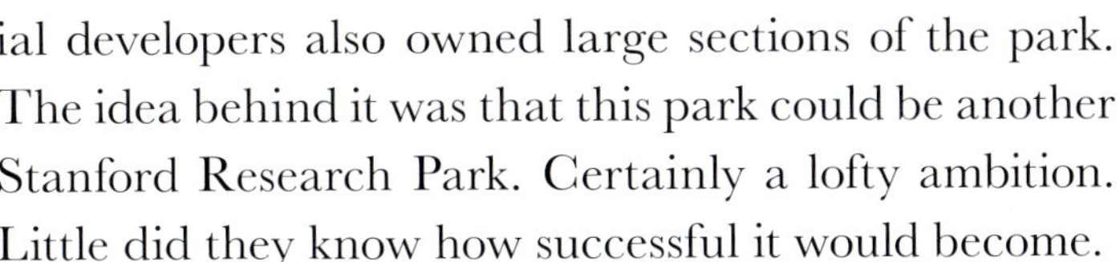

So we talked about how to give this park a big shot of business-vitamin B. The park had some challenges. The city dump was on the edge of the park. Access was a bit clumsy and there were no amenities in the park. However, it did have a golf course, well-laid-out streets, a Hollywood bowl kind of entertainment amphitheater, and developers that were creative deal-makers.

What we needed was to get people to put the park in their mind as a great place to build a company. Let's throw a BIG party and invite everyone… architects, designers, newspaper journalists, brokers. The challenge with this was: who would pay for this party?

The city had a budget of $7,000. I thought of the Bible story of the bread loaves and the fishes. Add to that we had no idea how many people would show up. It was October. So the theme was an Oktoberfest event. I found an accordion player. But how to get everyone looking at fifteen different buildings spread over fifty acres? I got the idea to get the developers involved by each contributing $1,000, and they each had to provide a broker treat to entice folks to see their building. I had lots of ideas for them.

One chose to man a coffee cart; one offered ice cream cones. One had a Mariachi band available and one handed out Halloween candy. The party was on. The market vacancy was 25% and the going rate was 85 cents per sq ft. Everyone knew we needed to do something. It was worth a shot to try this, even if it was a bit crazy. The city of Mountain View got the local newspaper to advertise it. Of course, I had found a lederhosen outfit to wear as my attire.

We set the October date and started the advertising to get people to come. This is always the most stressful part of any event. What if everyone thinks this is silly? (It was a bit silly. But we all were young and what else did we have to do? No one was leasing anything.) I visited brokerage houses, sent notices everywhere, and the 'party feel' started to vibe. At first it was just a hum. But after ten days, everyone was talking about it.

Long story short, we ended up with a huge crowd and people had a great time. We had changed the perception of the park. Tours picked up and some deals were getting signed.

Now an enormous rumor started: There was talk of Google going public. And on August 4, 2004, Google went public and the world changed. It was no longer a fledgling company. Now it was a well-financed public company with an incredible future ahead of them. And where were they located? Right in the middle of Silicon Valley on the edge of a beautiful park and the bay. The city of Mountain View got a steady stream of income from the leases to enhance the city that led to a new city hall, a library, improved schools—you get the idea. Google was changing the world one search at a time and Mountain View was a city on the rise.

I marveled at what a bit of enthusiasm, Irish luck, and risk to do something different could do. Then I went on to my next project. And I gathered armfuls of big scraps for my pile.

The city of Mountain View sent me flowers every year for five years, thanking me. I giggled. The magic ingredient wasn't me. It was Google. However, our timing could not have been better.

"YOU HAVE YOUR CHOICE OF AGENTS."

PLANTING MY STAKE IN PALO ALTO

In 2002, after twenty-two years in Santa Clara, I was now ready to make some changes. I thought I could hand over my book of business to my daughter, Diana. She was embarking on the endeavor of starting a family. And to whom would you trust your deals more than your daughter?

So I talked to the Palo Alto manager to let me move from Santa Clara to his office. After all, I was living in Palo Alto now. He was eager to hire some women in Palo Alto and my daughter was a perfect candidate… until she wasn't.

I moved in May. She was going to get her license to work in the office with me. Palo Alto was a halfway point for us. I started looking at the Palo Alto real estate landscape; I was learning 'Palo Alto.' For starters, when I left Santa Clara, I packed my boxes and carried them by myself to the car. I didn't have much paperwork to transfer. My skills were in my head, not in a file. When I got to the Palo Alto office, two young men rushed out to carry the boxes. Seemed like a small item but I thought, "Hmmm, this is different, polite, thoughtful, not the Wild West boys I'm used to." In Palo Alto, people played golf. In Santa Clara, people killed deer, rabbits, and ducks.

For starters, I walked around Palo Alto—shopping, restaurants, parks, lovely places to work. Santa Clara had an IHOP and a deli and a manicure salon two miles apart. Palo Alto was civilization in comparison. Then I drove around Palo Alto. Wow, much more densely located offices. Not all the driving I had to do in Santa Clara. Then I started recognizing neighbors. This felt really good. I liked it. I was the only agent ever to work in both Santa Clara and Palo Alto. However, I knew my work was cut out for me. I had to extend my Patty McGuigan brand into this new territory. I needed a project.

There was a four-building project on Geng Road at 101 and Embarcadero, that was built in the '80s, but vacant since the 2000 dot-com downturn. It looked old, unkempt, and unloved. I knew this was my stake. I could do something with this project.

Everyone in the office said the owner, Equity Office, never gave exclusives. I'd heard that before, but it did not stop me. I got the appointment to do a presentation. Game on!

I structured the presentation around the theme of Michael Lewis' idea in *Moneyball*. The way to fill this project was not with one tenant. By breaking the project up for smaller tenants, we'd win by walks and singles, not by home runs. I bought copies of the book, including book reviews, marked pages to read, and delivered the books two days before the presentation. They didn't have to read the book to get the theme.

I wrote a script for my team of three, complete with special boards that were hung as they gave their part of the speech. I had a printer do them so they looked quite professional. No one was reading a presentation or telling the story with a PowerPoint. This was a theatrical presentation with people moving around the room, placing placards with double-face tape at appropriate times as they talked. We practiced it until it ran like clockwork. It was good. Different. Dramatic. Well delivered.

We completed it with baseball hats with the project logo and baseballs suddenly rolling all around the table. We won the Oscar! We got the business. We began working on the project.

Next was the broker party to introduce the project to the brokerage world. I was in a baseball outfit topped off with an orange Japanese Giants kimono jacket and baseball earrings. I looked like a real fan. I had six-ft cardboard famous baseball personages leading down the road into the project as well as more cardboard players throughout the project. Then I created a path with baseballs all around the building… the path to lunch. Wildly successful, it was a new day for Geng Road in Palo Alto.

I must say these productions are always exhausting. When I got back to the office I flopped down on a chair to take a breather. Then I got a phone call from the police. Officer Martinez wanted to talk to the person in charge of putting these cardboard baseball players all around the city streets. I thought, "I've done it now. I'm going to jail for defacing city property."

He asked, "Are you planning to move these characters?"

"Yes sir, I will. I had a big party to introduce our new remodel of a real estate project."

"Well, where are you putting them?" he asked.

"I'll find a place," I answered, racking my brain about where on earth I could put them.

He said, "The fellows here at the station would really like them, if you don't have a specific use for them."

"Certainly sir. You can have them! I'll deliver them personally to the police department," I said. He answered, "That would be great." I was so glad not to be going to jail or be fined or in the papers as the woman that had defaced city property. I would have probably cooked hot dogs to go along with them, if they had asked me to.

The project turned a corner and we leased it up in record time. I had planted my stake in Palo Alto.

JOHN MOZART: THE PERFECTIONIST

John was another of the Magnificent Seven that grew up in Silicon Valley. He founded the Eurasian Automotive Parts Company, sold the business at a hefty profit, and turned to the real estate world, where he thrived on building well-designed buildings in premier locations.

About the same time he began real estate, he started collecting fine cars. His car collection is one of the very best in the country. He has built a museum for his cars and has the best of the best in it. John knows details about each of these cars that makes each one an amazing story. He would tell the tale of the car with all the enthusiasm of a sixteen-year-old driving his first car, except that he had hundreds of them with lots of stories.

When I was doing deals with John, his lobby would often be filled with packages from Sotheby's. I dreamed that in the next life I was to be a Sotheby's agent who was his personal shopper for unique stuff for his collections. That seemed far easier than the real estate deals I was doing with him.

John was a tough taskmaster in that he demanded the same intensity that he provided in getting a project done successfully. His razor-sharp eye wanted the best of me in my profession. He was the buyer extraordinaire.

John brought the same sense of detail to his real estate projects. Today, his Palo Alto building is the gold standard in class A office buildings.

I have leased buildings for John, sold him property for his housing adventures, and made money with him as an investor. Investing with him was the best part, because all I had to do was give him the money and I got to enjoy the profits.

"I HAVE A GOOD FEELING ABOUT THIS ONE."

SOMETIMES PRAYERS WORK

2008. I had been given the challenge of selling the Christian Science building, in essence a church. That year was also the year of the banking crisis. Silicon Valley thrives on crises and chaos. The rumor was that this was the Great Depression of our times. The sky was falling. Banks were collapsing. Lehman Brothers went belly up. Decisions got frozen, and I had a church to sell in the midst of all this turmoil.

This wonderful church structure, built in 1915, had the spirit of Mary Baker Eddy in it, along with no less than fifteen pictures of her. The building was historic; therefore, we could not alter the outside or change out the stained-glass windows. We could remove the pews. There was no parking. After all, God and his helpers didn't need cars and the church used the building only on Sundays. Yet the church was located right downtown and right across from city hall which had lots of parking. I had a perfect location with open space and great architecture. Off to find a buyer.

At first we had a venture capital firm interested. However, they proved not to have the money. Then I had a CEO come looking, but he had just been injured by an elephant on his African vacation and any stairs were a big negative for him. Finally, I found a developer with imagination and flair who was not afraid to take a risk: John Hamilton of Embarcadero Capital Partners. We created extra sq footage above the altar space, which can be perfect for something like an engineering collaboration lab. He asked, "Can you lease it?"

My answer: "Of course I can!"

We were in escrow but in the period called "the free look," which meant he could cancel at his whim… and the banks kept failing. He was going to have to find financing for this empty building, a real challenge. I knew I had to strengthen my case.

It was October—Halloween month. I ordered a nun outfit, then had our marketeers remove the Church of Christ lettering from the apron of the building on the brochure and put the name of the developer Embarcadero Capital Partners there instead.

I had a picture taken of the building. Then I took the picture to Baskin-Robbins and had a large flat sheet cake made with that picture on the cake.

I called John to make sure he'd be in his office. I headed up to his office in my nun costume, with Martinelli's, champagne, and the cake in hand. As I entered his office, I invited everyone to join us in the large conference room for a few minutes. We were celebrating John's new building.

People laughed, ate cake, and remarked how great the building was. I knew he would buy the building. He did buy it and then we leased it. To this day, John calls me Sista Patricia. And laughingly says, "I didn't buy this building, I was sold it."

Indeed he was.

THE SAN MATEO CORNERSTONE

While doing my Mountain View event that had revitalized Shoreline Park, Ellis Berns, the economic development director of Mountain View, and I had become great friends. In 2012, he retired. I was noodling over an idea about doing a creative project about Silicon Valley. He was interested in doing a video. I said, "Well, why don't we do something together and while we're doing it, we'll do some brokerage as well?"

His career had been in the public sector, mine in the private sector, which made a great man-woman team. What client could resist us and our wealth of knowledge? I showed Ellis how to cold-call. He explained to me all the vocabulary of city planning. He lived in San Mateo. My daughter lived there with three of my grandchildren—a good place to start our partnership.

I also knew a newly created development group, the Windy Hill Group, made up of three young men, two of whom I had worked with in my office. Ellis and I asked for a casual meeting, and chatting with them they pointed out the corner of 3rd Ave and El Camino, one of the cornerstones at the entrance to downtown San Mateo. "Find out about that lot," was Tod Spieker's comment.

I turned to Ellis. "So how do we find out about the lot?" In all thirty years of brokerage I had honestly never thought about a lot. I supposed they were saved for selling Christmas trees. Narrow thinking, I know. Was I wrong. Ellis looked up the owner info of the lot using city records and found the number.

I called the owner. We were off to the races. This ownership coincidentally was also a three-man partnership: a broker named John, a contractor, and another investor. My Irish luck played its part, I had called them at just the right time. Ellis had provided just the right questions and I added my sale spiel to the mix. Obviously, land is the first essential part to real estate and worth a good deal of money when it's in the right place at the right time. The land was worth $2 million. If you had the knowledge, time, money and skills, and were willing to take all the risks involved, you potentially could build a building that was worth $20 million.

John's office was located in San Francisco in the Tenderloin, a rough part of town. Finding parking and hoping my car would be there on my return were the first things on my mind. John was older and the business partners wanted to sell. John knew the value of a building at that spot, but for him that value would be split three ways and he'd be doing all the heavy lifting. "If I can get $2 million, I'll sell, but I don't want it to be tied up for a long time." Buyers want to "tie it up" (that means the buyer wants to control the ownership so you know you can build what you're dreaming of). We wrestled with pricing and timing, but we got to an agreement. My real estate sign went up on the vacant lot. I was now in search of the magic tenant who wanted 20,000 sq ft at the cornerstone of San Mateo.

Now, here is where one of my greatest real estate moments started. My grandchildren walked by that corner almost every day to get ice cream, or to go to the park or the toy store. They saw my name on that property for almost two years. You have to understand that in the minds of my grandchildren, if my name was on the sign, then I owned it. I did own it, but not how they thought that I owned it. I needed to lease or sell it. Once the entitlements were secured, the building started. My grandchildren were fascinated. I showed them the picture of what it would look like and asked that they tell everybody about it. You just never know where you're going to find your tenant. Then all their classmates and friends saw my name and the building in process. I became a real estate mogul in the eyes of five-year-olds. Finally someone in the family appreciated what I did for a living!

My favorite moment was when my first husband, who only knew me as a schoolteacher, was walking my grandson downtown past the building and Jack said to him, "That's my grandma's building. She's got buildings everywhere. She's famous." Jack has a very special place in my heart. There's very little he asks for that he doesn't get from his grandma.

So the building went up without a hitch. The city of San Mateo really liked the design and at long last a good-looking building was on the cornerstone to downtown San Mateo. We all did a walk through on its completion. Tod, one of the owners, brought his mother. I brought my grandchildren and their friends. Poppy, who really runs the family, walked through like a lender or city inspector. "Nice job, Grandma. This really looks good." I was so proud of myself I felt like I'd been awarded 'Broker of the Year.'

All of this because Ellis could find the phone number and I could get six men to agree. This was indeed one of my favorite scraps for my pile.

Then I realized I had really learned new skills. I no longer looked at lots as potential Christmas tree sites. I knew the vocabulary and uses for land. Even Poppy would say to me, "Grandma, there's a piece of land that needs your help." Any grandmother has to love that. I went on to sell six more land sites where over 1,000 housing units have been developed.

Now I'm intrigued with cemetery lots. That could be the highest and best-priced piece of land yet. Think about it—it's an evergreen business. People are always dying. Interesting as it is, there are still many challenges in the twists and turns of real estate today that I'm sure I can solve with a bit of creativity, some brashness, Irish luck, and an Ellis by my side to get me the phone number.

CHOP KEENAN: THE 8TH MAN

Chop Keenan was born in California with real estate in his DNA. His grandfather had built houses in San Francisco, and his father worked at Cornish & Carey Commercial in Palo Alto. Chop grew up in Palo Alto. He attended Menlo College, did a stint in the Marines, and fell into a job working for a title company. For two years he worked in an old-fashioned title company creating parcel maps with forty women. Building parcel maps meant putting little pieces of paper together to build each one. No technology to do that. It was all done by hand. But that seemingly monotonous, precise work somehow morphed into a deep understanding of how real estate worked. He was hooked and began building his "scraps" that turned into his real estate empire.

Chop is the face of the Peninsula. His playground is and was Palo Alto where he owns eighteen buildings. Chop loves Palo Alto.

He diversified to build a large Mountain View campus, two hotels, and multiple shopping centers. However, it was in a joint venture with Ponderosa Homes that he made his big splash. He had land to build 3,700 homes in Pleasanton.

Chop has built a "best-of-the-breed" portfolio of real estate through hard work, hands-on expertise, and a series of brilliant, instinctive entrepreneurial moves that turned his dream into reality. And, as the song from Evita goes, "the money kept rolling in."

LEARNING THE LANGUAGE OF LAND

The leasing market in 2016 was a bit slow, but residential land was the hot ticket item. Housing was in demand.

Silicon Valley was going through yet another transition. All these companies had hired lots of people and these people needed housing. Housing prices skyrocketed. There was a crying need for apartments, condos, townhouses. Density became the topic of the day. How high can you build? Silicon Valley did not want to turn into Manhattan. Height restrictions rose up in most cities. The very lay of the land with a bay on one side and the mountains and earthquake fault lines on the other controlled development.

No Los Angeles sprawl was going to happen here. The land simply did not permit it. We didn't see the larger issues of land constraints yet, but something was definitely afoot.

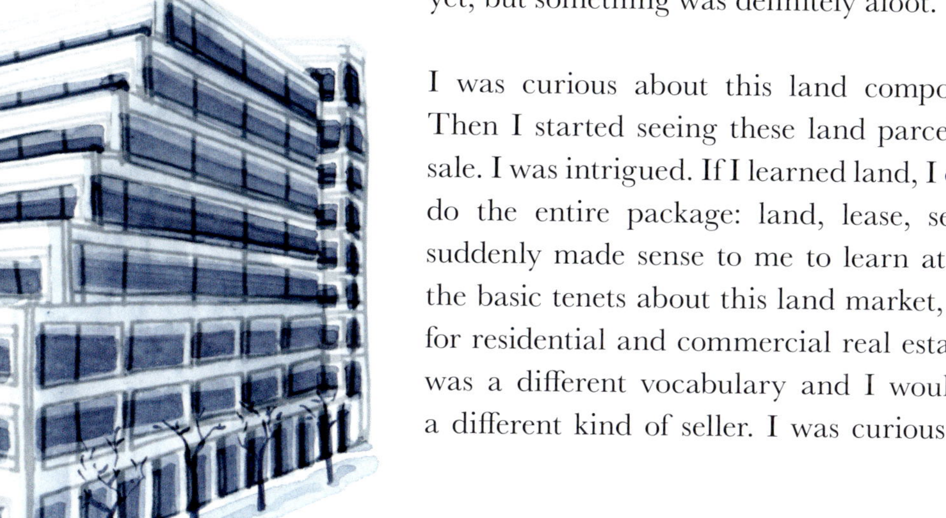

I was curious about this land component. Then I started seeing these land parcels for sale. I was intrigued. If I learned land, I could do the entire package: land, lease, sell. It suddenly made sense to me to learn at least the basic tenets about this land market, both for residential and commercial real estate. It was a different vocabulary and I would be a different kind of seller. I was curious how these deals were put together.

About the same time, I met a delightful man, Scott Ward, who headed up the residential land acquisitions for one of the well-known developers, John Mozart. Scott and I often ended up meeting for coffee in Palo Alto after my yoga class and we became fast friends. I found Scott fascinating. He was a kind, helpful gentleman with a wealth of knowledge. Scott was the only man I had ever met in the Valley that said, "I've made enough money." He was definitely his own man.

Scott was smart, had worked in the nonprofit world, had taken a run at developing housing that had not gone well. In John Mozart, he was meeting an extraordinarily successful commercial developer who sensed that a residential component could be a way to grow his portfolio. He recruited Scott and the two were phenomenally successful. And I got Scott as my teacher. We had a grand time.

Scott's wife was in New York studying nursing. He would go there at least once a month. I teasingly called myself his California girlfriend. His wife didn't mind as I was fifteen years older than Scott and happily married. So I'd find these land listings. I'd show them to Scott and he would explain the vocabulary, who a potential buyer might be, what was good about the piece of land, and then what it was worth.

In this process, I discovered this one piece of land in San Mateo. Scott said, "We might be interested in this piece of land." I did not know the first thing about writing up a land offer. Scott said, "No problem. I'll write it up. I know what we can do."

Lo and behold, this was turning into the makings of a deal. Scott, the buyer, was going to meet with the agent and seller the following week. My only challenge, I was going to be in Scotland when they wanted to meet. I told the agent that that day worked well for everyone but me, as I was going to be exceptionally busy, but I could call in. He said that would work and we set up the meeting. Scott, who knew me well, asked, "Patty, where are you going to be?"

I sheepishly answered, "Scotland, but I can call in." So I was in my hotel room with a glass of wine at 10 p.m. in Scotland and called into San Mateo where it was 2 p.m. In thirty minutes, terms were agreed to. Scott got the purchase offer drafted. Forty-five days later we closed the deal.

Now the little secret to that deal is that I had not seen the land. I knew San Mateo but not that street. When the location was mentioned I just nodded and said, "Great piece for a development," not knowing what kind of development since I hadn't seen the land.

I concluded that land deals were interesting and if the parties were sensible the deals were easy. I subsequently learned all the pitfalls and complications that can appear in later transactions. None were as much fun as that first one with Scott as my client. But I could add a new kind of scrap to my pile.

"YOU GET USED TO THE EBBS AND FLOWS OF THE MARKET."

SUNSET CASTS A NEW SHADOW

Sunset magazine was an icon of western living. Bill Lane ran the magazine from the late '50s until 1990. Lane and his brother took their father's $65,000 investment and turned it into an enormously successful publishing business worth millions. He built the headquarters on sixteen acres in Menlo Park on the corner of Middlefield and Willow. Once a year he celebrated 'Sunset days' there. He invited the public to see the magic of the magazine in action. New recipes were made and shared with the visitors, garden experts showed how to mulch and trim properly, and build a flower bed, etc. The 'Sunset days' became quite an attraction for homemakers from all over.

Sunset was a melting pot of creative ideas for food, garden, and travel in the west. Bill Lane believed the West was a can-do place. Little did he dream of what came next. People flocked to the two beautifully-designed California buildings to see the latest ideas in kitchens, homes, and gardens every October. However, time marched on. Bill Lane died in 1990. The business was sold to *Time* magazine, which then sold the buildings to a local developer. In 2016, the buildings had a new owner and were refurbished to work in our tech world.

One building became the headquarters for a young start-up company named Robinhood Inc. The young founders loved the bones of the building and were certain a tech company could function there. Robinhood was the typical fast-growing "unicorn" company, a name for companies that were privately owned and valued at over a billion.

One of the buildings, now occupied by Robinhood, had been sold as a typical leased investment to a large real estate investment firm, a rather standard kind of real estate transaction. The second building was empty. Not yet refurbished, and it needed to be leased or sold. However, the real estate story was a far more complex story that was atypical, involved, intriguing, and unique. But there were so many loose ends with this building that no local buyer wanted to touch it. There were no city approvals, it couldn't be built because of zoning, it was located on well water... so many complications.

On the other hand, this building was a grande dame, with a spectacular lobby, and glorious property (but the city had the right to walk on, so no development). I laughingly referred to it as the most expensive lawn in Silicon Valley. The layout was usable but it only had twenty-two parking places for a 47,000-sq-ft building. And it was on well water. It needed asbestos remediation. It essentially needed to be gutted. So I had to find someone to fall in love with this grand dame.

I managed to find a lovable Russian with a magnificent dream. He was the son of an oligarch and wanted to turn this into a gentlemen's club. I said we'd have to call it something different. Walking into the city of Menlo Park with an application to use this building as a gentlemen's club would have caused heart attacks around town. I said we should call it a world tech center for collaboration and creation (Irish creativity at work). This Russian was represented by a wonderful, hard-working Russian residential agent named Elizabeth Igudesman. Commercial agents are notoriously rude to residential agents, so no one gave us any credibility in trying to put this deal together. Add another small obstacle: our Russian spoke no English. I spoke no Russian. She was my savior.

Elizabeth and I became fast friends. We must have toured over one hundred Russian investors. Busloads came and we had real estate packages of information about the building, its potential, the market around it, and the history of Silicon Valley, hoping this would get someone interested in investing. Finally Elizabeth's oligarch agreed to buy it with all cash.

Now we had to deliver this Russian money, millions of dollars, to the owners. This was during the money crisis with Germany and Deutsche Bank. I read the *Financial Times* every day checking the Russian sanction list. Earlier, we'd had a potential investor, but he had been arrested in Nice.

I went to a Russian gathering and was to meet the premier of Kazakhstan. When I found out I was going to meet him, I got the atlas out to see where it was and its attributes. It's as big as Texas and loaded with natural resources. He was interested in having some engineers collaborate in Silicon Valley in order to diversify his economy, which made sense.

At one point, we did have one other investor put up earnest money. But after sixty days, he pulled out because there was too much risk.

This deal had all the trappings of a spaghetti western, borscht-style. The truth was, I could not dig up any other candidates, and this one potential builder loved the building. We finally pulled it off. Our buyer, the son of the oligarch, was on the global gold list of

Citibank. The money was wired and the deal closed.

I can honestly say, looking over my forty-four years of real estate, this was the wildest most unlikely deal I ever worked on. Sometimes I question, "Did this really happen?" It did close—no lawsuits, no drama. Robinhood, who had leased the first building across the street, by now desperately needed this building. They would do their own improvements.

I do believe Bill Lane is turning over in his grave watching the ups and downs of his beloved building in this crazy new century. I will say this: the building is well loved now, and it is beautiful.

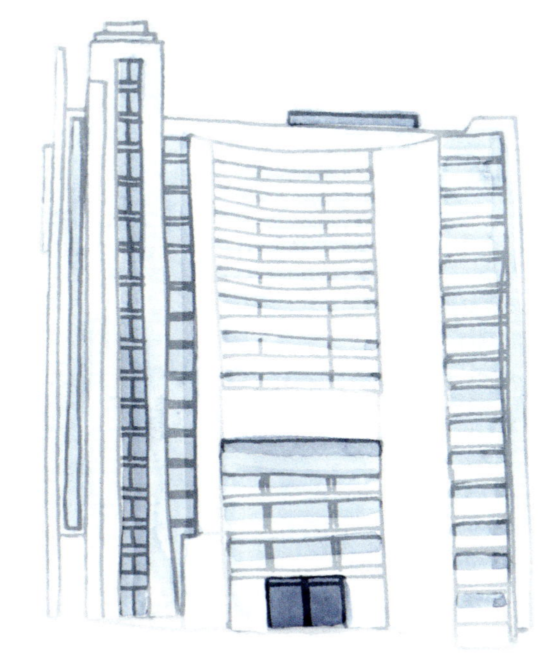

GOOGLE'S HIDEAWAY

I met this group as a referral from one of my favorite contractors, Larry Crawford. "This group," he shook his head, "They're not sure what they want, but they need you." I had to sign nondisclosure agreements. No one was to know who they were and what they were called. This was going to be fun. This was the first of what we today call a "family office." They were looking for 5,000 sq ft of secluded space in Palo Alto, where they'd have a quiet spot away from their company and with an outside space for dogs.

There were five of them on the first tour and on the next, there were seven. The group was growing. I found a secluded building in Palo Alto by Fry's, the electronics store of tech tools for engineers. It had a small, fenced yard and was all one story. Perfect. Now to get the lease signed. The landlord was a crotchety, retired developer that had little tolerance for these new young entrepreneurs. "Lots of crazy ideas if you ask me, this nonsense of a nondisclosure and no-name company. Give me three months' security deposit and don't bother the neighbors."

We gave him three months' deposit and did not bother the neighbors nor did we tell him we were Google. Everybody was happy, including the dogs in their own little yard.

When we got the building, Sergey Brin wanted to see the roof for

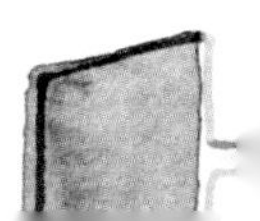

some reason I don't remember. I went up with him just in case he slipped. I'm not sure what would have happened if I'd slipped, but anyway, nobody slipped. So we were all okay after that little escapade. I had made an excellent new connection for myself.

In those days in Palo Alto the internet infrastructure was awful. So before I left them to it, it was decided that the Google's head of IT would come over to work his magic. While he was working on it, I casually let him know that my internet was awful at home as well and that I didn't live far away. After he got their internet working, he said, "I'll come and check yours out as well." So he drove his car over to my house to inspect our system.

My husband Richard came home and as he entered the house, he asked, "What's that red Maserati doing in the driveway?"

I casually said, "Oh it's the head of IT for Google, he's fixing our internet."

Richard said, "Okay then," and wandered back into the garage. Nothing I ever did surprised him and just maybe our internet would get repaired.

That deal was great fun on several levels, and many more were to follow.

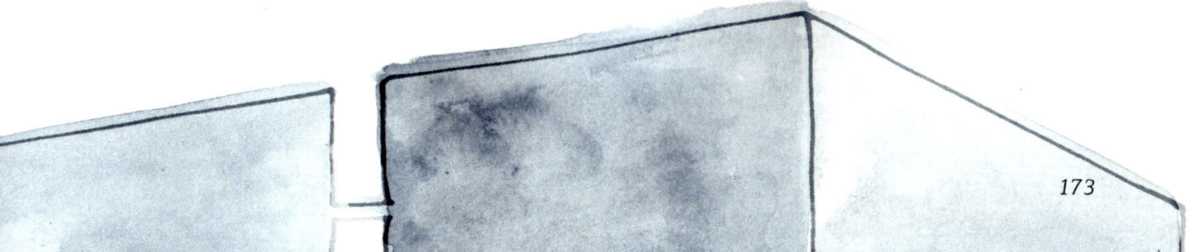

NEXT ASSIGNMENT: REDO A CITY

The Google boys split up as their private lives evolved. One group bought property in Los Altos and decided the city needed an upgrade, and they were just the ones to do it.

They hired a creative, delightful woman named Amanda Tevus whose career had been in retail brokerage. She had created Santana Row and updated Town & Country shopping center in Palo Alto, both highly successful retail projects. Now she had a new canvas to work with—the town of Los Altos. Noble goal but heated reactions from the town people because Los Altos folks liked their city the way it was. Friction arose but it did move forward.

There were five women in the development operation. I was the broker. I can honestly say this was one of my most fun brokerage experiences. It was like playing monopoly with real pieces. We built a breakfast spot so that women with children could come for coffee. It had a play area with supervised child care, and wine was served in the afternoon. We had a Western-themed jungle gym restaurant for a lunch spot with hamburgers and hot dogs, but we didn't bother with parking. The city revolted about that.

I sold them an antique store where I eventually bought multiple pieces of furniture along with an elephant as a tabletop decoration. The elephant would walk across the table playing "Happy Birthday." (I still use that for birthdays.) Then we bought an empty defunct restaurant. The antique store ended up providing spillover space and an extra refrigerator for the lunch spot. We were taking development down a whole new path!

One day, by myself, I went down the elevator in this empty building. To my dismay, the elevator doors on the garage level would not open up, and I was locked behind a gate to the garage yelling for help. Eventually a neighbor walking on the street heard me yell and saved me. After that I made the rule to never go into an elevator in an empty building ever again. That is a good rule to follow.

I leased another store to Steinway & Sons, the piano company, and got to meet the president of Steinway. I leased a bakery. We bought a furniture store and were in the process of converting it into a speakeasy in the basement with hamburgers on the ground floor and a bowling alley and milk shakes upstairs. However, before that came to fruition, everything came crashing down.

Our ex-Google construction group did a midnight move of sorts and moved up to a Northern California isolated ranch near Lake Shasta. All projects stopped. The city of Los Altos was in cardiac arrest, and the budget was totally wacked out. Reimagining the city of Los Altos was a wild wonderful adventure and some of our stores are still there. The idea of remodeling the city faded and life slowly returned to a quieter pace.

One wild crazy assignment in Northern California while it lasted. I loved every minute of it. Now it was back to office buildings and start-up spaces.

LIFE IN THE LOCKER ROOM

Our company was a sales force. We did not build a product. We were not a large corporation. We were not national. We were regional. For years we had two offices—Palo Alto and Santa Clara. Then we opened San Mateo and Sacramento. We yearned for a San Francisco office. Eventually we opened one in San Francisco, but the cultures never blended. We were not "city folks." We were Silicon Valley-ites. We belonged to the magic miles from Palo Alto to Santa Clara. San Mateo was the little kid up north and Sacramento was a bit too east. Santa Clara was always "Big Man" territory where men were men. Santa Clara hunted, Palo Alto golfed. Facility managers who played pool were replaced by CFOs as the decision-makers for real estate decisions.

As an entrepreneurial, small real estate company, we were simply organized. People and deals—that was our motto. We had no training programs, no employment contracts, no assistants. We had biweekly office meetings to share market information. Those were so funny they could have been a weekly comedy show.

We also had no HR department. I was walking up the stairs to one of the meetings when one of the fellows nudged me, "Good-looking calves, Patty." He was talking about my legs as he had looked at them up the stairs. I knew he meant it as a compliment, but it did remind me of something you might say at a rodeo about a horse walking around the ring, and it's something that would be taboo to say in an office today. Oh well, it was the only time someone has ever talked about my calves.

The nicknames that bantered around the office were certainly the rumbles and noise of a locker room. One fellow Jimmy was a master of the nickname. I was Fireball, Leona was Flawless. Her husband John was called Lucky John. My husband's last name was Bush. He was called The Bushman. My daughter's name was FB 2. She did not care for that. One fellow with no sense of humor whom Jimmy did not particularly like was called The Undertaker. Diane Talbert was Pompom.

Sadly Jimmy's talents and sales skills did not progress as the tech world moved forward. His formula for living his life was odd. We all were outgrowing the boy banter as entertainment. He ceased to entertain and became the brunt of office jokes. The transformation was cruel, nasty, and sad. He ended up leaving the office, and moving out of California. I hope his humor found an audience in a slower-moving world.

The swearing and cursing from a good portion of the men would have caused Paul Bunyan to blush. Periodically, a man would stand up and announce, "I'm going to Kerley's (a gun shop in Cupertino). Does anyone need any ammo?" I had gone to a parochial school for fourteen years, six of those years with all girls. I was always amazed by the behavior. I have worked as a coworker in an environment of 95% men for forty-four years. That daily environment certainly stripped me of some of my femininity. With this environment as my home court and the field of players as tenants—Chinese, Russian, Persian, Pakistani, Indian, etc.—you see the picture. This was a colorful, diverse, business environment to build my pile.

Colorful, different, never boring, all of this in an economic world of a digital revolution. No wonder I can't retire. There is never a dull moment.

THE GOLDEN TRIANGLE

If Palo Alto was the incubator for technology and Sandhill Road in Menlo Park was the financial district for the fledgling companies—the Golden Triangle is where the companies planted their headquarters, the area bound by the 101, the 17, and the 237. The idea of the Golden Triangle went back to the '80s, but really came to fruition in 1994–1995 when 237 was upgraded to an expressway. These three roads were the magic sides of this triangle. Inside this circumscribed patch of land, buildings mushroomed as tech boomed. Google, Apple, Microsoft, Nvidia, Intel, AMD, Intuit, 3Com, Cisco, National Semiconductor, and the list goes on and on. All grew their companies inside the Golden Triangle. Permits to build flew out of the city "planning" offices. Tilt-up walls appeared everywhere. Traffic became horrific. Freeways grew lanes. Astounding!

I remember on Tremble Boulevard and 1st Street, right in the heart of this Golden Triangle, was a slaughter house. I cold called on the owner. This was prime land for development. Buildings had gone up all around it, but the owner held out. I knew I could convince him to sell his property. I went to his office to chat with him about his business. He decided to give me a tour of the entire operation. Watching animals get slaughtered was a new experience for this city girl. I think he knew I was a bit innocent. After the tour, I knew I was not going to be the broker that got this man to change his mind. However, he eventually did sell, moving his cattle and his pots of gold south to Central Valley. Orchards disappeared. Enormous wholesale flower growers moved south or retired. Drive-in movie theaters were transformed to office buildings. Mortuaries and churches were fair game for development.

Fremont became the manufacturing haven for the tech world—Tesla, solar plants, Apple's first manufacturing plant, Seagate, Lam Research, and so on.

For me the Triangle was a perfect playpen. I couldn't get too lost where these boundaries and companies bounced around like popcorn—expanding, contracting, merging. The pace of the tech business cycle was brisk, no doubt about it. There seemed to be only two options—growth or extinction.

The San Jose airport expanded and became international. No one was singing "Do you know the way to San Jose?" anymore. San Jose was on the map.

And well, my pile was a mile high with thousands of scraps of various sizes. This was a candy land for a salesman. Lots of new companies emerging, a growing number of jobs, and IPOs were the belles of the stock market. The economy did have ebbs and flows.

We had dot-com booms and busts, tax changes, and interest rate fluctuation all causing a bit of chaos, but the intellect, curiosity, and sheer vitality of the place continued to make for an exciting wonderland to build a career. I can certainly attest to that.

ACADEMY AWARDS, SILICON VALLEY STYLE

As a broker, your relationships are your lifeline. Everyone develops their own style and selects a path that suits his or her talents. You do have to know the territory, understand the basics of business, and consistently "show up," but after that everyone's book of business becomes unique and as colorful as the broker themselves.

Silicon Valley is a continuous fountain of new ideas. Steve Jobs said, "Embrace every failure. Own it, learn from it, and take full responsibility for making sure that, next time, things will turn out differently."

Along with his "think different" motto, folks were given permission to create new products and change the course of people's lives. The spirit was contagious and attractive to so many people.

To quote a great friend of mine, Chop Keenan: "It is high-octane living here, and it's not for everyone. But if it works for you, it's exhilarating and rewarding."

Every year the Association of Silicon Valley Brokers (ASVB) comes together for a grand celebratory evening to honor developers and a variety of brokers in all categories. I have always seen many similarities between brokerage and Hollywood. You're your own standalone business though often you belong to a "community," a brokerage house or a filmmaking company.

Both are competitive, and you're only as good as your last deal or movie. Colorful, exciting, community-driven businesses. Relationship-oriented. Though both businesses are in different communities, Los Angeles and Silicon Valley are dominant in a multitude of ways. Not surprising that Barbie and AI technology developed where they did.

Once a year we celebrate and honor the brokers that have accomplished something special that year. That's when it's possible to pick up an ASVB award for achievement.

I can say I had one of those years in 1997; I was inducted into the Broker's Hall of Fame. That was quite an accomplishment. I was not expecting such an accolade. I was the first woman to join the Hall of Fame. That in itself was astonishing. Steve Moulds, who had hired me and had directed me in a superb how-to course in brokerage, handed me the award. It's always been one of the highlights of my career.

I've never confused myself with greatness or having been the largest dealmaker or the best in business. I was only focused on building my pile. However, this pile was getting to be a showstopper.

Now, when I go to the ASVB award ceremony, I see the evolution of our business to a far more corporate design. Certainly still a male-dominated business, still a critical part of the business world, but handled in a far more adult, sophisticated corporate manner.

No one is hiring gorillas anymore!

STARTUP CENTRAL

67 Evelyn Ave had all the ingredients for a startup spot: central location, close to the train, walk to downtown with a plethora of inexpensive restaurants, right off of the freeway, flexible size, many parking spaces, and 2,000 to 6,000 sq ft per individual company, very inexpensive. However, it wasn't perfect. There wasn't a window in the whole building.

Gil Eakins, the owner, bought the 30,000-sq-ft warehouse building with a funky second floor to house his company. He was an engineer from Rensselaer, a premier engineering school in upstate New York. He'd spent time in the Coast Guard and had come west to build his life. Gil was a man with drive, smarts, and a can-do attitude.

As the years rolled by, he developed separate-sized offices that were ideal for startups to incubate an idea. They generally had a conference room, a couple of offices, perhaps a lab area, a kitchen and bathroom, and nary a window. Why would anyone working there need a window? Their heads were always down developing an idea.

Gil's wife Sandy was smart, artistic, and active in the community. She had been mayor of Palo Alto, involved in the League of Voters, and the local art center. She brought a creative eye to the suites that made them inviting and unique. The property lot was oddly shaped so there was lots of parking plus an even odder smaller building that housed a paint company. Gil eventually bought that as a gym/ workout area for the building, and he stored his remodeled Model T cars there.

This building was not going to be up for any design awards any time soon. But it was certainly up for the job to be done by anyone who had an idea for a company. My husband alone started three companies in there. In one of them, he had a yoga instructor come at 5 p.m. on Tuesdays. In another, he had a country band come to celebrate an engineering breakthrough that advanced the product dramatically.

Once, one of the "presidents" (it's hard to think of that word with these young fellows) found Gil and asked him to put a door into the adjoining suite. Gil said, "No problem." He picked up a sledgehammer and started knocking out a door. The next day the ever-present Perfecto, a fabulous facility fellow who kept the building standing, came in and finished the job. No permit, no design. Door installed. Done.

Each company would "start up" in this kind of simple environment. Then, if all went well, they'd gather some more buddies, get some seed money from some venture capitalists, move to a larger spot, and grow a company.

Business at 67 Evelyn was like life on a carousel; up and down and around, testing your ideas, could you get the idea into a working product, was there a market for it? If all systems were a go, then off you went down the street or around the corner to another property to develop the next cycle in the company. In the '80s and '90s, ideas were everywhere. This was the process and this was the kind of building for it.

People did think differently back then. The word impossible did not exist, and the definition of failure was you'd learned something so the next time you did it better. I helped hundreds of those kinds of companies get their spaces. Some people called it work. I thought of it as an adventure in a new world.

MONEY

Venture capitalists have been around for centuries. In days past, they were the patrons of the arts, the robber barons. All kinds of wealth was made during different eras. But at the end of the 20th century, these folks would be called venture capitalists (VCs). They took the financial risk to invest in an idea. They found a concept that was daring and original, and provided the resources to make it all happen.

Young men were dreaming up seemingly wild schemes. These young companies they were founding were the beginnings of the rise of the digital age. Folks debate when this digital age actually started, but everyone knew by 1980 it was here.

A cluster of men would come together over an idea and find some seed money to test if it works. If it looked like the product or idea might work, they got more venture capital and built a company around the product.

The goal was to build a company that was profitable and then "take it public" and scale it—in other words, grow it. Many of these companies did not last long. They'd get bought. Or another idea would make them obsolete and they'd disappear. The tech business was a fast-moving world. Grow or die seemed the theme.

In the early days, the rule of thumb for "going public" was 100 million dollars in gross sales and profitability. The venture capitalists owned a good number of the shares and the employees got a number of shares depending on their time with the company and their particular skill level. The modern day gold rush was upon us.

Look at the Dow Jones Industrial Average over the decades:
1980. 963
1987. 2000 (Hitting 2000 was cause for a BIG celebration)
1990. 2633
2000. 10729
2010. 11577
2020. 30606

These numbers continue to be extraordinary and unheard of. Exponential wealth was amassed and the world changed. Silicon Valley became a force in the world economy.

The home court for the venture capitalists was located in Menlo Park on Sandhill Road. This was an unpretentious group of "woody walk-up" buildings, certainly nothing like the spacious skyscrapers of New York.

There was an atmosphere of collaboration, approachability, competitiveness yet supportiveness, youth and adventure for a seemingly endless flow of ideas in the technology world.

Steve Jobs was twenty-one when he founded Apple. Larry Page and Sergey Brin were in their twenties when they founded Google. When Sergey Brin and Anne Wojcicki were having their first child, everyone was invited for the baby shower and were to come in diapers or onesies. New York did not think like that. Few people thought like that. It's no wonder they didn't fear failure. They had just started their lives. New York thought about money. For Silicon Valley, they didn't have to think about money because the money came rolling in.

The venture capitalists' funds grew enormously and that started more companies. Other parts of the country tried to emulate the formula but to no avail.

In those days, the VCs did stay close to the company and did provide sage advice about growth and direction. They invested in what they could see and supervise and that formula seemed to work.

Groups would spring out of other groups and more companies would spring out of other companies. And real estate? Brokers provided the brick-and-mortar spaces to make the technology advances come true. There was no hybrid work then. Young people worked and played together for endless hours to complete or perfect an idea. The spirit was contagious, and my pile was growing amazingly. I had clients in all stages of development. In those years, among the awards I received was the Worn Shoe Award for the most deals for the year. It was the norm for me to do fifty to seventy deals a year.

By today's standards, life looked so simple and it probably was. However, it was so different from any other part of the country. Back then there was not yet the enormous gap between executives and workers. Everybody made money. Certainly, some more than others, but not like what happens today. In retrospect, while it was wild and crazy, it seemed somewhat balanced for everyone. We were busy, young, making money, building an industry, an industry that changed the world.

POWER

Electric power is the secret sauce of Silicon Valley. The chip is the basis of all technology. To build the chip, you need an inordinate amount of power. The more complicated the product, the more chips needed; the more complex the chip, the more power used.

Gordon Moore, a co-founder of Intel, predicted in 1965 that "the number of transistors on an integrated circuit (a chip) will double every two years with minimal rise in cost." Today the number of chips for an Apple watch would have run all of the Apple lab in the 1980s. That may seem like Greek to a non-Silicon Valley person, but it's the Bible in the Valley—speed and power run the place.

Santa Clara became the garden spot with land and cheap power. The city of Santa Clara has its own municipal electric utility, and the elected city council oversees policy and pricing. Since Silicon Valley Power is not-for-profit, it is able to keep rates lower than the competition without sacrificing quality and availability. At the time, little thought went into what this did to the land or the water. As the power needs grew exponentially for chip-making, other places became sources—the Columbia River in Oregon, Arizona, Taiwan. The industry also needed power for other parts of building a product. One example were clean rooms.

Another use of power was the server room. All those computers that sit on the desk need power. Sizes varied, but a server room became a staple of every real estate requirement. Then server farms came into existence. They are "a collection of computer servers generally maintained by an enterprise and/or hosting provider to accomplish server needs far beyond the capability of one machine." Server farms often have backup servers for redundancy in the event of a primary server failure. By this point in time everyone was quietly getting addicted to power. You see the "breakdowns" when the internet goes down are all about power.

Next was the cloud. I always think of this idea as my grandmother's attic. She had everything up there and so does the cloud. We now store files, pictures, movies, documents, etc. This is my vision of my grandmother's attic—seemingly endless storage. But we still need to have a router of some sort for our devices. It's all gotten very complicated and it all starts with a chip.

I have always thought the city of Santa Clara should have been the queen of the Valley, the crown jewel. The city has a power source, a mission, a marvelous university, perfect access to the airport, and an amusement park. Somehow, it has never been able to assume the authority to run the Valley. Today each city has its own strengths and challenges. But the Valley is the golden fifty miles and it does seemingly run the world with a high need for power.

Today, we're back again in search of power for the super computer for the AI explosion. Surprise! Creating AI takes an enormous amount of power.

Some say Google needs as much power to run its AI division as needed by the entire country of Ireland. Why the heavy power? AI processes an inordinate amount of data to connect all the data to the internet. Connecting all the information in the world and processing it so it's connected to the internet that delivers what information you need to the phone in your hand or the computer on your desk—well, it's a lot of work requiring a lot of power. Somehow that challenge will get resolved but you can see the constant demand for more power. And the beat goes on because money and power run the world.

It has now been over forty years since the onset of the digital revolution, which has transformed from a mere revolution into a powerful force shaping the global economy. Today, nearly everyone possesses a cell phone, which functions as a compact computer with capabilities exceeding those of the IBM mainframe from the 1980s. These devices are deeply embedded in our daily lives.

While money and power continue to drive the world, their meanings have evolved to include new dimensions. Entrepreneurs, innovative companies, and brilliant ideas continue to emerge; it has become an expectation in our society. Silicon Valley has developed into a commanding economy in the world. Gone are the days of simple baby parties; those children are now entering college, and their parents are firmly in middle age.

The Valley is characterized by its eclectic population, entwined in issues such as traffic congestion and housing shortages, while also grappling with global challenges like climate change. Innovations such as solar panels and solar farms have been developed, self-driving cars to alleviate traffic woes, and drones to address various challenges, including the search for new energy sources.

"THE COMMERCIAL REAL ESTATE BUSINESS ISN'T FOR EVERYONE."

SAME ANTICS, DIFFERENT PLAYERS

Fast-forward to 2025. We all think life has changed dramatically. The tech revolution was a moment in time to remember and smile and share. Yet I still work. I have 200,000 sq ft of multi-tenant office projects that I am responsible for. I lease space. Deals are still out there though not in the same volume.

In March, I got a call from Mary, a wonderful broker friend. She had a startup that needed 1,000 to 2,500 sq ft. What did I have? Of course, I had the perfect space. We all met at the lobby of a Palo Alto office building. There is at least two million sq ft of office space in all of Palo Alto with 25% of it vacant, but I told these fellows that right here in this building I could deliver for them the perfect space. Look no further. I spoke with perfect confidence as I showed them four spaces. At the last space, their eyes lit up. Indeed this was the perfect space, complete with desks, chairs, and a kitchen. They said, "You're right. We'll take it. We need it Monday." It was Wednesday. Now the magic of Silicon Valley pulls the rabbit out of the hat.

The space was a sublease from an enormous Chinese company valued at billions and headquartered in Beijing. The building was owned by another large Chinese company worth billions. The prospective tenant was a startup company funded by Andreessen Horowitz, one of the top prestigious venture capital firms. I think perhaps they were working in Andreessen's lobby.

The founders were two young men that looked like they might not be shaving yet. They would pay full price. They had raised 10 million—they showed us the bank statement. They wanted the space in three days and would pay all the rent up front.

Subleases are always problematic, more complicated, and take longer to complete. There are three parties rather than two involved in this transaction. The zinger—they only wanted it for six months and the landlord and sub-landlord were headquartered in China.

This was "Mission Impossible" and I suited up for it. We had to get company insurance. We accomplished that in six hours. For some unknown reason, the sublessor wanted 14 million worth of insurance. While it was an outrageous amount, the extra cost was $500. The tenant said, "We need the space." We got the additional insurance. Over the weekend documents flew across the Pacific multiple times through a fifteen-hour time difference.

Monday arrived. The documents were still getting finalized though all the business terms were agreed to. The sub-landlord said, "Fine. We'll get our end wrapped up, give them the key and let them move in." They moved in on Monday. Mission accomplished.

This group did have a sense of magic about them. I guarantee you a deal like this has not been done before, but it absolutely demonstrates the essence of the "Silicon Valley style" that still is alive and well. This kind of craziness only happens in the Valley.

As for me, my journey into the realm of commercial real estate here turned out to be an exhilarating and rewarding ride. It took grit, determination, a dash of imagination, and Irish luck to succeed in this fast-moving world, but I was up for the adventure. At times, my life has felt like a Hollywood movie—and I've been both the star and the director in a wild, action-packed blockbuster. And as the credits roll, I can only smile at the stories I've been lucky enough to tell. The reel keeps turning, and the adventure isn't over yet.

APPENDIX

Patty with her first car phone in 1984

THE TEN MOST WANTED LIST

Memorize these faces! They are wanted by a lot of people, particularly by those who have a complicated real estate transaction to put together. These are our Top Ten Producers for 1990. Give them a call. There is no substitute for success!

Shown left to right: (Bottom) Judy Herrington, Diane Talbert, Patty McGuigan. (Standing) Fred Pilster, Jack Troedson, Phil Mahoney, Howie Dallmer, Tim Swan, Randy Scott, Craig Brinitzer.

Cornish & Carey Commercial Real Estate

Santa Clara 4701 Patrick Henry Drive, Suite 2501 **408/727-9600**
San Mateo 901 Mariners Island Blvd, Suite 125 **415/341-5800**
Palo Alto 400 Hamilton Avenue **415/322-2600**
Sacramento 1601 Response Road, Suite 160 **916/920-4400**

The Five Faces of Success

Pictured from left to right: Kelly Nicholls, Jim Binsacca, Loren Toews, Fred Pilster, Patty McGuigan.

Despite a challenging year in commercial real estate, this incredible team of professionals from our Santa Clara office led our company towards a record 10.7 million sq. ft. in closed deals in 1992. With their unparalleled determination to succeed, no matter the circumstances, they have been able to accomplish the impossible. Cornish and Carey Commercial is pleased to recognize their diligence and pursuit of excellence.

Santa Clara Office 408/727-9600
Santa Clara • Palo Alto • San Mateo • Sacramento

If these were the Academy Awards, C&C just brought home Best Actor, Best Actress, and a Lifetime Achievement Award.

☆ Patty McGuigan, Cornish & Carey
ASBB Broker Hall of Fame

☆ Frank Cox, Cornish & Carey
ASBB Industrial Broker of the Year

☆ Diane Talbert, Cornish & Carey
ASBB Office Broker of the Year

The greatest honor in Hollywood is the Oscar. In commercial real estate, it is the ASBB award. In both cases, the awards signify their peers' recognition of outstanding work in their given fields. Furthermore, the awards recognize an advancement on a standard of excellence.

This year, three Cornish & Carey professionals took home ASBB awards. Cornish & Carey is truly proud of these individuals for their hard work and undying determination to succeed. Moreover, we are exhilarated to see that the real estate community is in full agreement.

Patty made "Realtor of the Year" fifteen times throughout her career

BEST OF THE BEST

It's a tough act to follow.

In a challenging year for commercial real estate, these five dedicated professionals garnered rave reviews for their contribution to Cornish & Carey Commercial deals totaling over 12,000,000 square feet. Their talent and commitment to success made this remarkable accomplishment possible.

We are proud to honor Cornish & Carey Commercial's Santa Clara Office Top Five Outstanding Performers for 1993: Jeff Rodgers, Christine Sahadi, Jim Binsacca, Patty McGuigan and Gary Dillabough.

CORNISH & CAREY COMMERCIAL

ONCOR INTERNATIONAL

SILICON VALLEY / SAN JOSE
BUSINESS JOURNAL

VOL. 21, NO. 52 APRIL 30, 2004

In Depth

INFLUENTIAL WOMEN in BUSINESS
REAL ESTATE

'Rain dancer' loves the game

Patricia McGuigan

BY RACHEL POST
sanjose@bizjournals.com

When Patricia McGuigan started in the commercial real estate business in the 1980s, she was one of the first women in her field. McGuigan, now a senior vice president at Cornish & Carey Commercial, has sealed some 50 real estate deals a year for the last 24 years. She's leased a number of locations that total over 1 million square feet.

"I've earned my walking MBA by working with every facet of the economic and business world," she said. "I've leased every major office space in the valley."

Her real estate clients range from start-up entrepreneurs to facility managers of major corporations to Israeli fighter pilots who've moved to the valley. "They're sending my name around the Israeli army now," she said with a hearty laugh.

'I'm a rain dancer, I get things going.'

Over the years, commercial real estate ownership has evolved as companies look for creative ways to organize their office space and facilities. McGuigan finds her larger clients have smaller footprints in Silicon Valley, but their outsourcing tentacles reach worldwide. She has also witnessed a change in the industry from entrepreneurial to institutionalized. A company's decision to lease a location has now become an integral part of their whole business plan.

It's incredibly important that a real estate agent understands the company and their goals, McGuigan explained. "Commercial real estate can enhance life or kill the business," she said.

One of the biggest gifts she gives to her clients is her time, she said. She describes herself as a person of boundless energy and enthusiasm. "I'm a rain dancer," McGuigan said. "I get things going."

McGuigan loves meeting different people and hearing their stories. She makes a point of talking to five people she's never met before at every event she attends. By being able to cross reference people and their businesses, she gains insight that can be very valuable to her clients.

"I think it's a wonderful rule that every woman should follow," she said. "I like playing the game."

RACHEL POST is a freelance writer based in the East Bay.

SILICON VALLEY / SAN JOSE
Business Journal

CRE Quarterly

January 22, 2010

Veteran brokers steer next generation toward success

BY DAVID GOLL

Mary Blaser is no stranger to the commercial real estate business. She worked in high-profile marketing and management positions for ProLogis and Deutsche Bank, but when she joined Cornish & Carey Commercial in 2008, it was in a new career as a broker.

"It doesn't matter what kind of background you have, when you move into a new job like this, you start with a clean slate," said Blaser, a Santa Clara University graduate and senior sales associate at Cornish & Carey.

Blaser had considered moving into a broker's job for years and finally did so just as the industry began its current decline. She started working at Cornish & Carey's Santa Clara office in September 2008, the same month the financial crisis became apparent to most Americans as the stock market plummeted.

"It actually was the perfect time to start because I didn't know any different," Blaser said with a chuckle. "The first year was definitely a challenge, but it turned out I did very well. I got a lot of inspiration from Patty."

Patricia McGuigan, a 30-year veteran in the industry, has served as Blaser's main mentor as she made her mid-career job transition. McGuigan, a senior vice president based in Cornish & Carey's Palo Alto office, continues to inspire and motivate Blaser, as do other more experienced company colleagues.

Key to success is mentorship

Although common in many career fields, mentorships — known as "runnerships" at Cornish & Carey — are viewed as crucial for the success of new brokers in the competitive world of commercial real estate.

"It's really an invaluable relationship when you start out," said McGuigan, who spent her first 22 years with Cornish & Carey in its Santa Clara office.

McGuigan also had a mentor in Steve Moulds, former chief of that office who later became executive vice president/partner at the company.

VICKI THOMPSON

AWAY IN: Mary Blaser, right, began her career as a broker at Cornish & Carey Commercial just as the market started to decline. Within a year, with the help of Patricia McGuigan, left, the duo had closed the sale of a $2.4 million, 5,600-square-foot building in Sunnyvale.

'You can really flounder out there if you don't have that kind of help and guidance.'

Patricia McGuigan
Senior vice president,
Cornish & Carey Commercial

"You have so many questions, even on the definitions of terms used in the industry," she said. "You can really flounder out there if you don't have that kind of help and guidance."

Now that Blaser is more established, though still on a steep learning curve, McGuigan said the support has become reciprocal.

"I've mentored many newcomers to our company over the years, but there comes a point when you begin learning as much from them as you are imparting," she said.

Blaser said McGuigan has helped her not only with some of the basics, but with new career skills, as well.

"Patty is really an entrepreneur," Blaser said. "My previous job experience trained me to manage things and take care of details on the technical side. She has taught me the tricks of the trade, and I'm learning to become much more of an entrepreneur myself."

McGuigan and Blaser collaborated on several deals together during 2009.

Blaser said the largest was a $2.4 million sale at 1560 Sunnyvale-Saratoga Road in Sunnyvale. The 5,600-square-foot professional building was sold in July. She said they represented the seller as well as the buyer in that deal.

They also worked together to help Gain-

SILICON VALLEY'S Women of INFLUENCE

SPECIAL SUPPLEMENT · MARCH 19, 2010

Private Sector

reflects the immense volume of information that exists, and the scope of Google's mission: to organize the world's information and make it universally accessible and useful.

Residence: Palo Alto

Education: Bachelor's in symbolic systems and master's in computer science, Stanford University; honorary doctorate of engineering from Illinois Institute of Technology

Boards/volunteer work: Mayer has taught introductory computer programming classes at Stanford to more than 3,000 students. Stanford has recognized her with the Centennial Teaching Award and the Forsythe Award for her outstanding contribution to undergraduate education.

Cheree L. McAlpine

General counsel, Wyse Technology Inc.

Wyse Technology is the global leader in thin computing-based virtualization software and hardware solutions. Wyse and its partners deliver innovative hardware, software and services that optimize cloud computing, virtualization and green IT.

Residence: Danville

Education: Suffolk University Law School

Boards/volunteer work: Omnipeace Inc. and Sacred Heart Community Center

First job: Weil, Gotshal & Manges

Business heroes: Warren Buffett, Oprah Winfrey, Sam Walton

Proudest achievement: My daughters and my support of Panzi hospital (for female victims of violence) in the Democratic Republic of Congo

Biggest workplace challenge: Creating more opportunities for women and minorities in the legal profession

Five-year goal: Finish my book

Patty McGuigan

Senior vice president, Cornish & Carey Commercial – Palo Alto office

Cornish & Carey Commercial is a full-service commercial real estate company operating in eight Northern California locations. The company is owned and operated by its top executives and employs more than 240 people.

Residence: Palo Alto

Education: Bachelor's in English, UCLA

Boards/volunteer work: Board member of the Palo Alto Art Center; member of the Palo Alto Chamber of Commerce; member of Commercial Real Estate Women Network and the Association of Silicon Valley Brokers

First job: Teaching high-school English

Business hero: Katharine Graham, publisher of The Washington Post

Proudest achievement: Two children through college in four years with 3.5 GPAs

Biggest workplace challenge: Staying positive

Something that would surprise others: I'm a flamenco dancer and piano player.

Five-year goal: Write a children's book with my grandchildren as the characters

Debby Meredith

Venture partner, JAFCO Ventures

JAFCO Ventures is a venture capital firm investing in emerging technology companies. We look for exceptional companies with differentiated technology and compelling business models. We lead expansion-stage venture financing, and, since all of our team has both significant venture capital and operating experience, we are able to help businesses scale to their potential.

One of my most interesting jobs was being a lumberjack.

Lorrie Norrington
President, eBay Marketplaces, eBay Inc.

Residence: Los Altos

Education: B.S. with double major in computer science and mathematics, University of Michigan; M.S. in computer science, Stanford University

Boards/volunteer work: Board of trustees, Computer History Museum; founder, Los Altos Community Foundation

First job: Member of technical staff at Bell Laboratories in New Jersey

Business hero: Although Microsoft was a fierce, some may even say unfair, competitor while I was at Netscape, I admire Bill Gates. Bill is an amazing technologist, entrepreneur and businessman, who is now a philanthropic role model.

Proudest achievement: Shipping several versions of the Netscape Navigator browser, which had a huge impact on the Internet, while at the same time raising two young girls

Biggest workplace challenge: Silicon Valley and the businesses I ... changing te... product exe... environmen... the same tim...

Something ... was previou... time I was t...

Five-year g... other succe... time helpin... to college.

Education ...

Boards/vo... Advocates ... tion's first p...

First job: A... in Santa Ma...

Business h...

Proudest a... sion trips fo... best educati... 30+ years o... fessional ex...

Biggest wo... law professi...

Something ... first sprint ... group (60-6...

Five-year g... disadvantag... a sense of t...

KidsPark is a national chain of hourly, drop-in, licensed childcare centers for 2- to 11-year-olds. Open days, evenings and weekends, it is a solution for both parents and children — kids enjoy the recreation program, and parents have peace of mind.

Residence: Los Gatos

Education: B.S., Indiana University, Bloomington; MBA, University of Puget Sound

Boards/volunteer work: Girls for a Change, Karmanos Cancer Institute

First job: Soda jerk at an ice cream/candy store

Business hero: Paul Newman for Newman's Own

Proudest achievement: Identifying hourly, drop-in childcare as a specialty niche and seeing it become a mainstreamed service with KidsPark as the largest national provider.

Biggest workplace challenge: Continued expansion in an economic climate where startup loans are hard for independent franchisees to secure.

Something that would surprise others: I scheduled the production of the monkeys for the children's game,

eBay, the world's largest online marketplace, and PayPal, which enables individuals and businesses to securely, easily and quickly send and receive online payments.

Residence: San Jose

Education: B.S. in business administration, University of Maryland; MBA, Harvard Business School

14

Patty McGuigan

Senior vice president, Cornish & Carey Commercial – Palo Alto office

Cornish & Carey Commercial is a full-service commercial real estate company operating in eight Northern California locations. The company is owned and operated by its top executives and employs more than 240 people.

Residence: Palo Alto

Education: Bachelor's in English, UCLA

Boards/volunteer work: Board member of the Palo Alto Art Center; member of the Palo Alto Chamber of Commerce; member of Commercial Real Estate Women Network and the Association of Silicon Valley Brokers

First job: Teaching high-school English

Business hero: Katharine Graham, publisher of The Washington Post

Proudest achievement: Two children through college in four years with 3.5 GPAs

Biggest workplace challenge: Staying positive

Something that would surprise others: I'm a flamenco dancer and piano player.

Five-year goal: Write a children's book with my grandchildren as the characters

ACKNOWLEDGEMENTS

"No man is an island, entire of itself." So spoke John Donne. And I can say with certainty: no author creates a book alone.

My push to follow the urge to write came during the pandemic, after my husband died. I had a big house, no husband, and my business had shut down for Covid. What was I to do? I knew I wanted to write—but not alone. So I commandeered my friend Marian to write a children's book with me, featuring our grandchildren as the heroes. I was off to the races.

Since then, six books have followed. I've had the joy of working with three co-authors (Marian, Tesha, and Ann); my soul sister Maria, who makes everything gorgeous and perfect; Ann, who ensures it's readable; Kate, who tidies us up; Rebekah, who brings our characters to life; Priska, who captures their emotions with magic; and John, who draws the funniest cartoons. Caitlin gives the books presence and stature in the world, Janis lights up our social media, Julie is our tireless marketeer, and Diane makes sure our books get into readers' hands.

The list could go on. We are a team of creative, joyful folks who love building a different world to share with our readers—and we have a marvelous time doing it.

A special thank you to the Silicon Valley real estate community, who provided me with a fertile and fantastical playground to revel in.